FUEL CELLS

Edited by

G. J. YOUNG

Alfred University
Alfred, New York

A Symposium held by the Gas and Fuel Division of the American Chemical Society at the 136th National Meeting in Atlantic City

REINHOLD PUBLISHING CORPORATION
NEW YORK
CHAPMAN & HALL, LTD., LONDON

Preface

The continuing quest for new and improved energy converters has greatly increased the interest in fuel cells in recent years. Indeed, the research of some of the contributors to this volume has provided, in part, the impetus for the renewed activity in a field that had received only casual study for over a century.

Within the last few years, the subject of fuel cells had been discussed in general terms at a few scientific meetings and isolated papers had been presented. However, there had been no attempt to hold a symposium which would include contributions from a number of prominent scientists active in the field or to publish a group of papers which would present a detailed picture of the present state of development.

In view of this, a symposium on fuel cells was organized and held by the Gas and Fuel Chemistry Division of the American Chemical Society at the 136th National meeting in September 1959. This volume contains the papers presented at the symposiun as well as a brief summary of the panel discussion that followed the invited contributions.

The great interest expressed by many organizations and individuals and the rapid advances in this field in the past few months strongly suggest that other symposia on fuel cells will be held by the Gas and Fuel Chemistry Division in the future.

Alfred, New York
June, 1960

G. J. YOUNG

Contents

Preface.. iii

1. INTRODUCTION, *H. A. Liebhafsky and D. L. Douglas*............ 1

2. THE HYDROGEN-OXYGEN (AIR) FUEL CELL WITH CARBON ELEC-
   TRODES, *Karl Kordesch*.................................... 11

3. CATALYSIS OF FUEL-CELL ELECTRODE REACTIONS, *G. J. Young
   and R. B. Rozelle*.. 23

4. ELECTRODE KINETICS OF LOW-TEMPERATURE HYDROGEN-OXYGEN
   FUEL CELLS, *L. G. Austin*................................ 34

5. THE HIGH-PRESSURE HYDROGEN-OXYGEN FUEL CELL, *F. T. Bacon*.. 51

6. HIGH-TEMPERATURE FUEL CELLS, *G. H. J. Broers and J. A. A.
   Ketelaar*... 78

7. CARBONACEOUS FUEL CELLS, *H. H. Chambers and A. D. S. Tantram*... 94

8. NATURE OF THE ELECTRODE PROCESSES IN FUEL GAS CELLS, *E.
   Gorin and H. L. Recht*.................................... 109

9. MOLTEN ALKALI CARBONATE CELLS WITH GAS-DIFFUSION ELEC-
   TRODES, *David L. Douglas*................................ 129

10. SUMMARY OF PANEL DISCUSSION............................ 150

INDEX.. 153

1. Introduction*

H. A. Liebhafsky and D. L. Douglas

General Electric Research Laboratory
Schenectady, New York

A fuel cell is an *electrochemical device* in which the chemical energy of a *conventional fuel* is converted *directly and usefully* into *low-voltage direct-current* electrical energy.

The length of this definition shows that the fuel cell problem has changed since the days of the catchier phrase "electricity direct from coal." The phrases italicized above need further discussion.

Electrochemical devices, rather than batteries, to differentiate fuel cells from the usual primary cells or storage batteries. In such batteries, the chemical energy to be converted is stored in the cell. Fuel cells, on the other hand, are bare converters that ideally will produce electricity so long as fuel and oxygen (air) are supplied.

Conventional fuels to eliminate the costlier materials. For present purposes, conventional fuels are the fossil fuels, including the naturally occurring gaseous hydrocarbons, or substances easily derived therefrom. Hydrogen qualifies if it is not so pure as to be prohibitive in cost; carbon monoxide which can be made from coal as water gas containing hydrogen, or as producer gas by the reaction of carbon dioxide, also qualifies. Under the present definition, oxygen or air is the only oxidant.

Directly and *usefully* imply that the device has an anode at which fuel is oxidized and a cathode at which oxygen is reduced (Figure 1-1), and indicate that the conversion proceeds at voltages not greatly below open-circuit, and at reasonably high current densities.

Low-voltage direct current to emphasize that the electrical energy thus produced differs from that commonly generated and transmitted. The electrochemical industry is of course a large consumer of low-voltage direct-current electrical energy.

In the simplest fuel cell (Figure 1-1) coal is supplied at the anode, where

* In writing this brief introduction to a symposium in a field that is changing much more rapidly than ever before, the authors have had to express opinions and to rely heavily on experience transcending their own.

1

it interacts with oxide ions to form CO_2 and releases electrons to the external circuit. These electrons do work on the way to the cathode, where they are captured by oxygen from the air. The oxide ions thus formed complete the circuit by flowing through the electrolyte to the anode. With oxide ions carrying all the current, and with their production and consumption in balance, the electrolyte remains invariant.

Advantages

Inherent simplicity, obvious from Figure 1-1, makes the fuel cell attractive. But even more attractive is the directness with which it converts chemical energy into electrical energy. As a consequence the Carnot-cycle limitation does not apply, for the energy being converted is never randomized as heat.

A better answer to why we want fuel cells is that they are potentially *convenient* and *low-cost* sources of electrical energy. As qualities making for convenience, the following were chosen (somewhat arbitrarily):

(1) High power in unit volume
(2) High power in unit weight
(3) Quietness
(4) Cleanliness
(5) Operation on air
(6) Fuel replenishment possible

Not all fuel cells promise the above advantages to the same degree, but the fact that fuel cells as a class can offer such advantages explains the cur-

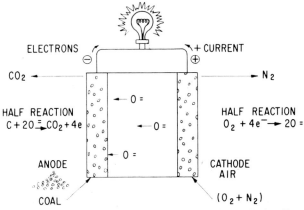

Figure 1-1. Schematic carbon-oxygen direct fuel cell.

rent interest in these power sources. Whenever reactants and containers must be considered in arriving at power in unit volume or weight, the efficiency of the fuel cell during practical operation becomes of primary importance as it determines the weight of reactants required for a given amount of electrical energy produced.

The possibility of fuel replenishment marks a distinction between fuel cells and conventional batteries. For short periods, conventional batteries are generally superior to fuel cells, which come into their own when electrical energy is required over long periods—periods long enough to necessitate continuous feed or replenishment of fuel.

The minimum cost of electrical energy from fuel cells is uncertain because the cells have not yet been developed to the point where this cost can be estimated reliably. The following factors are representative of those making for low cost:

(1) high efficiency
(2) low fuel cost
(3) low capital investment
(4) long life
(5) low upkeep

Low fuel cost is largely determined by high efficiency provided low-cost fuels are used. In fuel cells that develop large amounts of power at low cost, it should eventually be possible to attain over-all efficiencies exceeding the 40 per cent now realized in the best steam turbine-alternator plants. Fuel cell efficiencies taken alone however can be misleading. An over-all efficiency of 90 per cent sounds impresssive but is scarcely worthwhile if it is achieved only at current densities so low as to be impractical. Obviously, the current densities significant here are those attained under operating conditions.

Low capital investment, long life and low upkeep are particularly uncertain today for large fuel cells.

Origin

In a postscript added in January, 1839, to a paper in the *Philosophical Magazine* dated the previous December, Grove described an experiment in which a galvanometer was "permanently deflected" when connected with two platinum strips, both in contact with the same dilute sulfuric acid, the one also in contact with hydrogen, and the other also in contact with oxygen. On the basis of this experiment alone, Grove could scarcely be regarded as having invented the fuel cell. His intent from the beginning however was "to effect decomposition of water by means of its composition." This early intent and the remarkable 1842 paper in which he carried it out are sufficient to justify naming him originator of the fuel cell. Today these two inversely related electrochemical processes are being considered for energy storage.

In the later paper, Grove decomposed water electrolytically using 26 of his fuel cells in series as the power source. He proved that 4 such cells in series would decompose aqueous potassium iodide. The two electrolysis experiments can be considered the beginning of a practical electromotive force table. But the keenness of Grove's insight is best demonstrated by the following quotation, which indicates the difficulty of achieving high-current density in a fuel cell using gases: "As the chemical or catalytic action . . . could only be supposed to take place, with ordinary platina foil, at the line or water-mark where the liquid, gas, and platina met, the chief difficulty was to obtain anything like a notable surface of action." This same difficulty exists today.

For a hundred years after its origin, the fuel cell was the object of intermittent attention. Although no historical account will be attempted, two things must be mentioned. An address by Ostwald[1] shows that the fuel cell was clearly understood and thoroughly appreciated in 1890. A lifetime of devotion to the fuel cell by Baur ushered in the unprecedented research and development activity in the field today, and the review by Bauer and Tobler[2] will remain one of the classics in fuel cell literature.

Classification

The chapters which follow will show that there are many fuel cells. These cells could be classified according to their developers, the fuel used, the temperature of operation, and in other ways. The following calssification however is most useful.

(1) Fuel cells for special applications.

(2) Fuel cells for central-station power.

Convenience is usually the primary consideration in fuel cells for special applications; cost is secondary. "Special applications" are numerous and diverse: space vehicles, automobiles, and locomotives are only a few of many uses.

Cost will usually be the primary consideration in fuel cells for central stations (not necessarily stations that produce alternating current), although there may be an occasional large-scale installation for which cost is secondary. A successful central-station fuel cell is the most difficult to develop, but this application is well worth considering if only as the limiting case in which all the factors making for low cost will need optimization. The development of such a cell today is much more difficult than at the turn of the century when the over-all efficiency of steam plants was only about 10 per cent. Today, a central-station fuel cell would probably operate at temperatures above 500°C, have an electrolyte of molten carbonates, and a silver-containing cathode. Electrolytes in which oxide ion transfers the current (Figure 1-1) would have to operate at temperatures considerably above those for carbonates.

The above classification leads to several important conclusions about fuels. Ony a fuel carbonaceous in part can be low enough in cost for the central-station fuel cell. For special applications, hydrogen or hydrocarbons other than natural gas (propane, butane, kerosene) can be used; methyl alcohol or similar materials may also be used. For the central station, only natural gas (methane), water gas, or producer gas seem to qualify. Coal and residual oils should not be considered for direct use in fuel cells today because cells using these fuels cannot meet the requirements of a successful fuel cell (see p. 8). Fuel cells using carbon (Figure 1-1) can be run at high temperatures in the laboratory.

Ideal Efficiency

High efficiency is not always the primary advantage of the fuel cell. Efficiency warrants discussion in any case because it is important in order to understand the thermodynamics of fuel cells.

Consider the reaction

$$\text{Fuel} + \text{oxygen} = \text{oxidation products} \qquad (1)$$

Reaction (1) is intended to apply to any fuel discussed, and always to 1 mole of the fuel (e.g., 12 g of carbon or 2 g of hydrogen).

The first law of thermodynamics tells us that energy is conserved, that

$$\text{Work done} = \text{decrease in internal energy less heat liberated} \qquad (2)$$

In a system operating at atmospheric pressure, the work, $P\Delta V$, done by or on the system is conventionally separated from any other kind of work because such $P\Delta V$ work is not "useful." Once this separation is made, the first law reads

$$\text{Useful work done} = \text{decrease in heat content less heat liberated} \qquad (3)$$

In the case under consideration, useful work is electrical work.

If Reaction (1) is carried out under a boiler, no useful work is done, so that

Boiler: Decrease in heat content = heat liberated   (4)

The boiler has randomized the chemical energy of Reaction (1) as heat. The amount of heat produced is equal to the change in heat content during the reaction.

Heat, being random, cannot be converted to work unless the Carnot-cycle price required by the second law is paid. To be converted into electrical work, heat must flow from temperature T_1 to temperature T_2, and the maximum electrical work recoverable is $\Delta H(T_1 - T_2)/T_1$.

The first and second laws define the maximum useful work ΔG that can be recovered from a chemical reaction proceeding isothermally and reversibly. Perhaps the most important relation in chemical thermodynamics is

$$\Delta G = \Delta H - T\Delta S \qquad (5)$$

in which the incremental value of each of the three thermodynamic functions G (free energy), H (heat content) and S (entropy) is fixed by the properties of the substances involved in the reaction. The term, $T\Delta S$, is the heat exchanged with the surroundings. The application of Equation (5) to Reaction (1) proceeding isothermally and reversibly in a fuel cell is a vital part of this discussion.

For reasons not considered here, all fuel cells currently considered promising reject heat even when operating isothermally and reversibly. This fact is important for the following reasons.

(1) Heat is rejected because of the nature of the reactions at the electrodes.

(2) Heat thus rejected need not be wasted. It is potentially more valuable, the higher the temperature at which the cell operates.

(3) When heat is thus rejected, ΔG in Equation (5) is numerically smaller than ΔH.

On the basis of Equation (5), the ideal efficiency of the fuel cell is

$$\eta_i = \Delta G/\Delta H = 1 - (T\Delta S/\Delta H) \qquad (6)$$

It is less than unity, even in a cell operating reversibly, when heat, $T\Delta S$, is rejected.

The electrochemical cell is a remarkable and valuable device because it can convert chemical energy directly into work, thus bypassing the wasteful intermediate conversion to heat. There is an important relation

$$\Delta G = -E_r It \text{ (the minus sign is arbitrary)} \qquad (7)$$

between the maximum useful (here, electrical) work ΔG and the reversible electromotive force E_r. In this case, E_r is the electromotive force of a fuel cell in which Reaction (1) is being carried out isothermally and reversibly to deliver a current I for the time t required to consume 1 mole of fuel. The ideal efficiency (Equation 6) may now be written as

$$\eta_i = -E_r It/\Delta H \tag{6a}$$

E_r is the driving force that sends the electrons from anode to cathode in Figure 1-1. Each electron takes this path only once, in contrast to the conventional alternator where rotation through a magnetic field forces the same stream of conducting electrons to flow continuously through the external circuit.

Actual Efficiency

In a fuel cell under load, the actual electromotive force E_a will drop below E_r (Equation 7) for some or all of the following reasons.

(1) An unwanted reaction may occur at anode or cathode (or elsewhere in the cell).
(2) Hindrance to reaction at anode or cathode.
(3) Concentration gradients in the electrolyte.
(4) I^2R heating in the electrolyte.

The first two reasons enter into the reactivity requirements; the third is not usually serious, and the fourth is discussed in the following paragraphs.

It is advisable to define actual fuel-cell efficiency η_a. According to the first law, Equation (3),

$$-E_a It = \Delta H - q \tag{8}$$

where E_a is again arbitrary. The heat rejected, q, will be larger than $T\Delta S$ in Equation (5), owing to the factors making for irreversibility discussed earlier. The actual efficiency is

$$\eta_a = -E_a It/\Delta H \text{ (cf. Equation 6a)} \tag{9}$$

Note that this efficiency refers to the fuel cell alone and not to a system of which the fuel cell is a part. Here, as with η_i (Equation 6), ΔH includes the heat of condensation of water for cells in which liquid water is formed, but ignores it when the steam can be utilized.

The ratio E_a/E_r, which decreases with an increase in current density, is a convenient index of irreversibility. Values of 0.70 for this ratio at acceptable current densities (above 100 amp/sq ft on a central-station scale) should eventually be attainable. The difference between q and $T\Delta S$ is of course another measure of irreversibility; the lower η_a, the greater this difference. It may sometimes prove advisable to operate at low current densities in order to raise η_a to a value at which no special provision need be made for the rejection of heat.

Even though I^2R heat need not be wasted, it is often useless and can be harmful. In order to minimize it, the electrolyte must have high ionic conductivity with electronic conductivity absent, and the electrodes must be close-spaced.

Requirements

The diversity of fuel cells obviously makes it impossible to discuss in detail the requirements for each. It is possible, however, to give the principal requirements that an ideal fuel cell should meet. Such requirements fall under two main categories, as follows:

(1) Reactivity requirements
    (a) Proper stoichiometry
        H_2O and CO_2 only reaction products
    (b) High and unimpeded electrode reactivity
        High current density
        $E_a/E_r \simeq 1$
(2) Invariance requirements
    (a) No corrosion or side reactions
    (b) Invariant electrolyte
    (c) No change in electrodes
    (d) Long life

E_a and E_r are the actual, and the reversible electromotive force of the fuel cell as described above.

Fuel cells can of course be successful even if they do not meet these requirements completely. For example, a hydrocarbon such as propane need not be oxidized completely at the anode if fuel cost is unimportant and if incomplete oxidation does not develop into intolerable difficulties. Or, an electrolyte might be permitted to change composition if the change is so slow as not to interfere seriously with operation of the fuel cell.

The second reactivity requirement has engaged the attention of fuel cell investigators perhaps to a greater extent than any other. The problem here is to get a high rate of reaction (high current density) at the anode and at the cathode without unduly lowering the electromotive force below the reversible value. (See discussion on ideal and actual efficiencies.) This problem has long been recognized as one of the most important in electrochemistry. In fuel cell work, attempts are made to solve it by increasing surface (especially by increasing the extent of the gas-electrolyte-electrode interface), by raising the temperature, by increasing pressure, and by using catalysts. It is worth emphasizing that catalysts need not show the same order of effectiveness in a fuel cell as in a thermal reaction, e.g., in the anodic oxidation of a hydrocarbon as in catalytic cracking. Electrons are withdrawn or added at a fuel-cell electrode in a manner foreign to a thermal reaction; in a fuel cell, the catalyst is part of the electrical circuit.

The use of suitable intermediates to meet the second reactivity requirement is worth reviewing because it holds out the hope of high current density at low temperatures without risk of "drowning" the electrodes. The intermediates form oxidation-reduction couples, represented as $X^{++} - X$ and $Y^= - Y$. They operate as follows:

$$\text{Fuel} + X^{++} = X + \text{Oxidation products} \tag{I}$$

$$X \text{ (at anode)} = X^{++} + \text{Electrons} \tag{II}$$

$$\text{Oxygen} + Y^= = Y + \text{Oxide ion} \tag{III}$$

$$Y \text{ (at cathode)} + \text{Electrons} = Y^= \tag{IV}$$

These equations are not balanced, and the charges on the ions have been assigned arbitrarily. For the scheme to succeed, all the reactions must be rapid and remain in phase. Use of these redox couples must necessarily lower the reversible electromotive force below the value of E_r for Reaction (1); this can be a serious factor when fuel-cell efficiency is important.

The reactivity requirements are easiest to meet when hydrogen is employed as fuel. Carbon monoxide and the heavier hydrocarbons (propane and kerosene) are slower to react than hydrogen. Methane appears to be the most inert of the gases. Coal or carbon reacts sluggishly and has a tendency to reduce the electrolyte.

The invariance requirements follow from the statement that the fuel cell is an energy converter, and that such a converter can continue to function indefinitely only if it undergoes no significant progressive change.

The third requirement is intended to include both chemical and physical changes. Electrodes, especially gas-diffusion electrodes, often have small pores of carefully controlled sizes, the purpose being to increase current density by increasing the interface gas-electrode-liquid electrolyte. Such electrodes "drown" if the pores fill with electrolyte or with water produced in the fuel cell reaction. Although "drowning" can be controlled, the risk of its occurring makes solid electrolytes (such as ion-exchange membranes) more attractive.

Outlook

The current increase in fuel cell activity, if maintained, makes it likely that fuel cells will serve as power sources in special applications within the next five years. Successful, practical model cells are already in use. The future of central-station fuel cells cannot be predicted today.

References

1. Ostwald, W., *Z. Elektrochem.*, **1,** 122 (1894).
2. Baur, E.. and Tobler, J., *Z. Elektrochem.*, **39,** 169 (1933).

2. The Hydrogen-Oxygen (Air) Fuel Cell with Carbon Electrodes

KARL KORDESCH

Research Laboratory
Union Carbide Consumer Products Company
Division of Union Carbide Corporation
Parma, Ohio

Introduction

The reversal of water electrolysis on platinum electrodes in the first hydrogen-oxygen cell was demonstrated by W. Grove in 1839.[1] Early theoretical publications appeared shortly after 1900. Very extensive competitive efforts to build practical fuel cells started after World War I, ending in the mid-thirties without practical results. The improved heat engine, in spite of the efficiency limit set by Carnot's cycle, discouraged all efforts to construct fuel battery power plants. It is beyond the scope of this chapter to cover all the various fuel cell constructions tried during this period. For a comprehensive summary, see the review written in 1933 by Baur and Tobler.[2]

Practical oxygen-carbon electrodes became well known from experiments with air-depolarized zinc batteries. Around 1930, G. W. Heise and E. A. Schumacher at the National Carbon Company (now Union Carbide Consumer Products Company)[3] constructed long lasting air-depolarized cells with caustic electrolyte, more powerful than the earlier cells which operated with ammonium chloride. But not before 1943, when Berl published his studies,[4] was the peroxide mechanism of the carbon-oxygen electrode accepted.

After World War II scientists became strongly aware of the need to preserve fossil fuels by obtaining higher energy conversion efficiencies and research on fuel cells was revived.

Again it is impossible to cover all the progress made in recent years on

11

the many different fuel cell systems, but fortunately most communications have been collected in survey publications and papers.[5, 6, 7]

As far as the carbon electrode fuel cell is concerned, Davtyan in Russia[8] experimented with catalyzed carbon electrodes with unconvincing results. Justi in Germany[9] worked initially with carbon, changing later to porous metal electrodes. The lack of durable catalysts and good carbon materials was obvious. The high pressure cell of Bacon seemed to be the only prospective fuel cell.[10]

In the meantime, realizing that the simplest gas element was a carbon electrode cell operating at room temperature on air, Marko and the author, at the University of Vienna, investigated catalyzing procedures which led to high current oxygen electrodes for alkaline cells.[11] A short time later, Kornfeil,[7] Martinola,[12] and Hunger[13] joined the research group. The performance of hydrogen-oxygen carbon fuel cells looked very promising, but it was still difficult to obtain reliable carbon material.

In 1955 the author joined the National Carbon Company and was able to avail himself of that company's experience in carbon production. Together with R. R. Witherspoon and J. F. Yeager the present fuel cells have been developed.

Technical descriptions of the performance of practical hydrogen-oxygen batteries were presented by Evans at the Twelfth and Thirteenth Annual Power Sources Conferences of the U. S. Army Signal Research & Development Laboratories.[5] The papers by Evans discuss the features which are important in judging the merits of a fuel-cell system:

(1) Simplicity of the low temperature-low pressure cell.
(2) Availability of cell components and fuels at a reasonable cost. Carbon is a relatively cheap material of low specific weight.
(3) Convenient operating conditions and low maintenance requirements.
(4) Operating life.
(5) Power output per unit weight and unit volume: The maximum wattage output of all fuel cells is obtained around 0.5 volt. The highest fuel efficiency is realized at the highest possible cell voltage. The factor obtained by dividing the cell voltage by 1.2 gives the efficiency, e.g., 0.9 volt/1.2 volt = 0.75, or 75 per cent fuel utilization based on available free energy. For this reason a fuel-cell system should only be considered in connection with a specific application. A low current density, highly efficient system is more economical than a high current, low efficiency system if the operational period between refueling is long, in the order of months, for instance. The

possibility of waste heat rejection might also play an important role in selecting the best operating level.

(6) Overloading should not harm the cell. The carbon electrodes described in Evans' papers tolerate several hundred per cent overload for short periods. The speed of water removal in the system determines this property.

The fundamental principles and the performance parameters of cells will now be stressed.

Characteristics of the Union Carbide Fuel Cell

The construction of a laboratory-type hydrogen-air fuel cell with two concentric electrodes is shown in Figure 2-1. The electrolyte is 30 per cent KOH. The cell produces electricity as soon as the hydrogen is fed into the inner porous carbon tube. The outer tube is exposed to air. With more

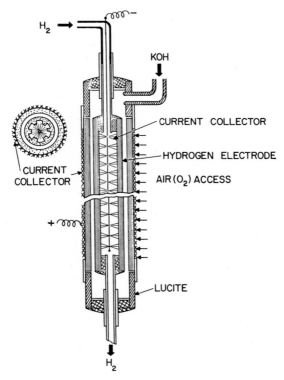

Figure 2-1. Concentric hydrogen-air fuel cell.

cells in series a common electrolyte circulation system is provided to remove water or carbonate if necessary. It should be noted that the CO_2
pickup from the air is astonishingly slow. In working with air-depolarized
cells, it was noticed that the carbon electrode effectively hindered carboniza-
tion of the electrolyte by the CO_2 from the air. With 20 per cent carbonate
in the KOH electrolyte, operation is not impaired after two years. The
larger surface of the outer tube offsets the lower current density of the air
electrode. With pure oxygen-hydrogen cells equal-surface electrodes are
preferred in order to obtain proper cell balance. Tube bundle cells or plate
cells are chosen in this case.

The Oxygen Electrode. Transportation of oxygen through the wall of
the carbon tube determines the current of the electrode. Fick's law for
linear diffusion allows a calculation of the pressure drop between the gas
side and electrolyte side of the carbon wall.[7] Under a number of operating
conditions, it amounts to several per cent of the applied gas pressure, depending on the load. No gas escapes into the electrolyte in a cell that is
operating properly. The pore structure is chosen such that a large pressure
differential is required to produce gas bubbles on the electrolyte-carbon
interface. Penetration of the electrolyte into the carbon is effectively
stopped by a special carbon repellency treatment.

The oxygen molecule adsorbed on the carbon surface is ionized in accordance with the two-electron transfer process:

$$O_2(\text{ads.}) + H_2O + 2e^- \rightarrow HO_2^- + OH^- \tag{1}$$

When special peroxide decomposing catalysts are used the hydrogen peroxide concentration is reduced beyond the sensitivity of analytical tests to
an estimated value of 10^{-10} molar. Catalysts suitable for this purpose, for
instance the very effective Co-Al or Fe-Mn-Ag catalysts, are described in
the patents by Marko and Kordesch.[14] The low concentration of peroxide
corresponds to the open-circuit potential of 1.10 to 1.13 volts against the
hydrogen electrode in the same electrolyte. The oxygen formed by decomposition of the H_2O_2 is entirely reused. This fact changes the two-electron process to an apparent four-electron mechanism. The 0.1 volt difference to the open-circuit potential of the oxygen-water electrode (1.23 volts)
reveals that the electrode is *not* following the equation

$$O_2 + 2H_2O + 4e \rightarrow 4OH^-$$

The hydrogen peroxide mechanism on carbon electrodes was also con-
firmed by Yeager and co-workers.[15] The temperature coefficient of the
oxygen electrode open-circuit potential is -1 mv/°C (negative). Under a
load condition of 10 ma/cm^2 we found a positive coefficient of $+0.75$ mv/°C

for the oxygen electrode increasing with the load.[12] The measurements have been obtained from O_2 | KOH | zinc cells; the zinc coefficient has been eliminated from the data.

In accordance with the theory, the oxygen electrode potential must be dependent on the alkali concentration of the electrolyte. The pH function is shown in Figure 2-2. Most of the measurements were made against a HgO reference electrode. The slope of the oxygen H_2O_2 electrode curve is about 30 to 32 mv per pH unit, in good agreement with the postulated value of 29 mv for a two-electron process. In solutions containing less than 0.01 N caustic, the potential values are not reproducible. The nonlinearity at higher caustic concentration is a direct measure of the activity coefficient. The abscissa indicates normality of the KOH, determined by titration with 1 N sulfuric acid.

The potential of the oxygen-carbon electrode follows the Nernst equa-

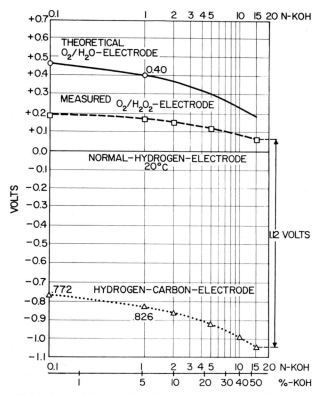

Figure 2-2. pH-function of Union Carbide type oxygen and hydrogen electrode.

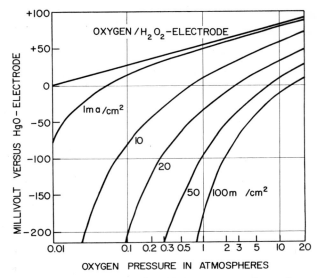

Figure 2-3. The potential of Union Carbide type oxygen electrode as a function of pressure.

tion. As a result, such electrodes can be used for determination of oxygen partial pressures. The practical usefulness of such electrodes for oxygen-sensing elements is increased extensively by the fact that a 1 ma/cm² load does not cause marked deviations from this behavior in the range between 0.1 to 10 atm pressure.[16] Total pressure changes give the same indication as partial pressure changes on open-circuit measurements but not under heavy load conditions. In the latter case the diffusion through the blocking inert gas causes an additional pressure drop across the carbon electrode wall.

Figure 2-3 shows typical pressure curves of oxygen-carbon electrodes, measured against an HgO reference electrode.

The effect of hydrogen peroxide concentrations in the electrolyte has been studied by Yeager and co-workers[15] and recently again by Vielstich.[17] The influence of the pH value of the caustic electrolyte on the hydrogen peroxide decomposition with and without catalysts was studied by Hunger[13] and led to the remarkable result that a minimum half-decomposition-time of peroxide is observed around pH 14. This effect might be explained by the increased ion mobility in highly concentrated caustic solutions. At higher temperatures the minimum tends to disappear, with rapidly increasing H_2O_2 decomposition values. Different catalysts change the half lifetime several magnitudes but the minimum remains in the same pH region. In strong caustic solutions only the best catalysts are useful. No catalyst was found under pH 13 which prevented a rapid increase in H_2O_2 half-life to values one hundred and one thousandfold that at pH 14.

The Hydrogen Electrode. Hydrogen is not active on untreated carbon electrodes as shown by careful experiments with carbons free of heavy or precious metals. For hydrogen electrodes we deposit a catalyst on the electrode surface. Metals selected from the Pt-group work best.

The reaction occurring at the catalytically active sites of the hydrogen electrode can be represented by the equation

$$H_2 \text{ (gas)} \rightarrow 2H_{\text{(ads. on catalyst)}}$$

$$2H(\text{ads.}) + 2OH^- \rightarrow 2H_2O + 2e^-$$

As with the oxygen electrode, the structure of the hydrogen electrode is important for the best gas diffusion rate. A permanent three-phase zone, solid/gas/liquid, has to be established by wetproofing the carbon material. In addition precautions have to be taken against "internal drowning" of the H_2-electrode by water formed during the reaction. As indicated by the equation above, water forms at the anode and this creates a second current-limiting situation, at least at low temperatures. (Water-removing measures will be discussed later.)

The hydrogen electrode also follows the theoretical pH function very closely as is shown in Figure 2-2. The good reproducibility of measurements makes the carbon-hydrogen electrode a tool for determination of activity coefficients. Electrode equilibria are reached in minutes instead of hours as required with the Pt/Pt black electrode.

It is not easy to poison carbon-hydrogen electrodes. In four years' of experimental testing of hydrogen electrodes, no electrode failed as the result of catalyst poisoning, except for experiments in which large amounts of cyanide were deliberately introduced. Oxygen is detrimental only if mixed into the hydrogen in such quantities that large amounts of water form catalytically. This catalytic recombination feature prevents accumulation of a dangerous gas mixture above the electrolyte. This is important in case of accidental gas leakage.

The open-circuit potential has a small negative temperature coefficient. Under load the voltage increases rapidly with temperature, especially in the range between 20 and 70°C. For example, at 0.85 volt cell voltage, the current density increases from 25 to 50 ma/cm².

The pressure sensitivity on open circuit follows the Nernst equation.

Under heavy load conditions, the pressure effect is magnified because of the faster gas diffusion and higher adsorption values reached under pressure.

Removal of Reaction Water. In principle there are four ways to dispose of the reaction water:

(1) Operate at a temperature near or above 100°C, in the latter case under higher pressure.

(2) Operate at low temperatures under reduced pressure, current densities at 100 mm Hg are above 20 ma/cm² at 0.8 volt.

(3) Use the gas-circulating principle. Water from the electrolyte evaporates through the porous carbon wall especially if a temperature difference is set up. The water removal speed depends also on gas flow rates and is limited by the saturation value of water vapor. With a cell temperature of 70°C and a condenser temperature of 20°C, 180 g of water is transferred by each cubic meter of gas streaming through the electrodes. Evaporation of water occurs at both electrodes; however, there is more water at the anode if the cell is operating.

(4) Operate at low cell temperatures, allowing all water to enter the electrolyte, with concentration of the electrolyte in a separate thermal or low pressure unit. For low power applications considerable dilution of electrolyte can be tolerated. The cell operates as well in 20 per cent KOH as in 50 per cent KOH. For example, a 1-amp cell can be operated for 1000 hr and produce less than 1 lb of water.

Cell Geometry. Because of the many possible fuel cell constructions, a comparison of different electrode arrangements and cell constructions had to be made. Figure 2-4 shows five basic arrangements of electrodes used in fuel cell constructions. The two-electrode tube cell (A) is the laboratory test cell model. Several hundreds of these have been built to test electrode performance. The other constructions show remarkable improvements as can be seen from the table in Figure 2-4. The empirical current factor used in this comparison represents the lower average polarization achieved by a more uniform potential distribution in the cell. The influence of ohmic resistance variations is eliminated by using the pulse current technique.[19] This method made comparison independent of the distance between the electrodes.

The improvement factor in respect to current output per unit volume or weight is more spectacular than the polarization drop mentioned. Cell D. for instance, is ten times more efficient in volume utilization than type A, The internal resistance is a major factor to be considered in high current cells. Cell E is many times better than type C at 100 ma/cm² current densities, but the difference is negligible at 10 ma/cm². The above exam-

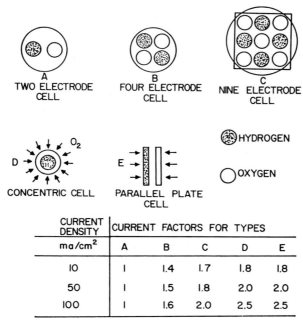

Figure 2-4. The effect of cell geometry on the current output of a cell.

CURRENT DENSITY	CURRENT FACTORS FOR TYPES				
ma/cm^2	A	B	C	D	E
10	1	1.4	1.7	1.8	1.8
50	1	1.5	1.8	2.0	2.0
100	1	1.6	2.0	2.5	2.5

ples show how important the engineering of fuel cells for special applications can be, independent of electrode performance.

Performance Characteristics. Figures 2-5 and 2-6 show the voltage/ current curves of hydrogen-oxygen-carbon fuel cells under different conditions. The ohmic resistance is again eliminated by means of the pulse current (interrupter) technique.[19] All curves on the graph can be compared on an equal polarization basis. To calculate actual terminal voltages in special cells the following values should be used:

Electrolyte resistance: 1.0 to 2 ohm cm (depending on temperature and concentration)
Electrode spacing: 0.1 to 0.3 cm

For example, the voltage drop due to the ohmic resistance in cell components is about 0.02 volt at 100 ma/cm^2 for a parallel plate battery. The terminal voltage of the cell can now be determined by combining this internal resistance loss with the appropriate polarization value from Figure 2-5 or 2-6. In practice, this means that the curves in Figure 2-5 are

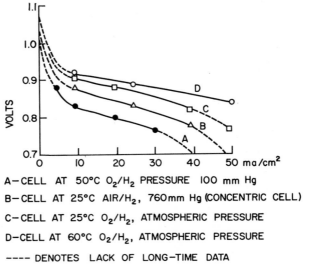

A—CELL AT 50°C O_2/H_2 PRESSURE 100 mm Hg

B—CELL AT 25°C AIR/H_2, 760mm Hg (CONCENTRIC CELL)

C—CELL AT 25°C O_2/H_2, ATMOSPHERIC PRESSURE

D—CELL AT 60°C O_2/H_2, ATMOSPHERIC PRESSURE

---- DENOTES LACK OF LONG—TIME DATA

Figure 2-5. Performance parameters of Union Carbide fuel cells.

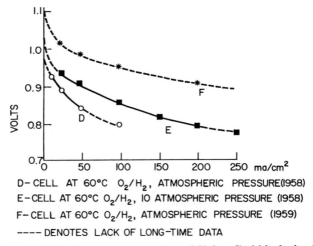

D—CELL AT 60°C O_2/H_2, ATMOSPHERIC PRESSURE(1958)

E—CELL AT 60°C O_2/H_2, 10 ATMOSPHERIC PRESSURE (1958)

F—CELL AT 60°C O_2/H_2, ATMOSPHERIC PRESSURE (1959)

---- DENOTES LACK OF LONG—TIME DATA

Figure 2-6. Performance parameters of Union Carbide fuel cells.

very close to terminal voltage curves; the curves in Figure 2-6 due to the high current density should be corrected in accordance with the chosen cell construction.

Life Expectancy. Low temperature, low pressure cells are not subject to electrode attack by electrolyte or oxidation. The only life-limiting factor is wettability of the carbon electrodes.[18] The tendency of the electrode to wet appears to depend on the potential at which the electrode operates rather than the current density at which it operates. Two years of intermittent service have been achieved on 10 ma/cm² and over one year of continuous service on 20 ma/cm² at 0.8 volt, with tests still in progress. This has been achieved at atmospheric pressure, between room temperature and 70°C. In the meantime, better repellency treatments and more active catalysts have brought performance up to 30 to 50 ma/cm² at 0.8 volt for at least the same time period. The use of increased pressure gives the benefit of very high currents at low temperature, but creates a greater need for auxiliary equipment. The operation of completely "wet" carbon electrodes under high pressures might give the additional advantage of reducing maintenance and control devices very considerably.

Special Fuels. Hydrogen is an ideal fuel. One-eighth of 1 lb produces 1 kwhr in a fuel cell. Hydrogen in liquid state can be stored for months, with a container weight approximately that of the hydrogen weight.

For everyday purposes, hydrides, decomposed by water, are a more convenient choice. One pound LiH is equivalent to 1 kwhr.

To be practical, a fuel cell must operate on air, be inexpensive and use a readily available fuel. Our cells operate with high current densities on air with only a small potential difference to the pure oxygen-hydrogen cell. The use of carbonaceous fuels (liquids or gases) at low temperatures is one of the goals which we are attempting to accomplish. Good results have been obtained with alcohols, carbon monoxide and aldehydes but the need to remove carbonate from the alkaline electrolyte complicates these systems.

The use of catalytic chemical converters to produce hydrogen from hydrocarbons looks promising. The present oxygen-carbon electrode does not function well in acid. The use of a redox-chemical intermediate (e.g., bromine) is necessary for high current outputs.

All halogens operate on carbon electrodes with high current densities in acid systems. As a result hydrogen-chlorine fuel cells can operate at high power outputs for extended periods. Despite the higher voltages and high current densities which can be achieved in hydrogen-chlorine fuel cells, the energy output per pound of combined fuel is less than that of the hydrogen-oxygen cell (because of the low equivalent weight of oxygen).

Future Outlook

It may safely be assumed that the fuel cell will eventually become a major power source, replacing other systems in some applications. For the immediate present, fuel cell applications will probably be restricted to those in which the excellence of fuel efficiency, silence, freedom from fumes, simplicity of design and operation are important requirements.

References

1. Grove, W. R., *Phil. Mag.* III, **14,** 129 (1839).
2. Baur, E., Tobler, J., *Z. Elektrochem.,* **39,** 148–180 (1933).
3. Heise, G. W., Schumacher, E. A., *Trans. Electrochem. Soc.,* **62,** 383 (1932); *ibid.,* **92,** 173 (1947); *ibid.,* **99,** 191 (1952).
4. Berl, W. G., *Trans. Electrochem. Soc.,* **83,** 253 (1943).
5. Proceedings, Twelfth Annual Battery Research and Development Conference, U. S. Army Signal Research & Development Laboratory, 1958 Symposium on Fuel Cells. Proceedings of Thirteenth Annual Power Sources Conf. of the U. S. A. S. R & D Lab., 1959 (in print).
6. A review of the State of the Art and Future Trends in Fuel Cell Systems, Office of Naval Research, Cont. Nonr 2391 (00), 1958, by E. Yeager, Western Reserve University, Cleveland, Ohio.
7. Kornfeil, F., Survey of Galvanic Fuel Cells, AIEE Conference paper 56-327 (1956), F. Kornfeil, Dissertation, University of Vienna (1952).
8. Davtyan, O. K., *Bull. Acad. Sci. USSR, Dept. Sci. Technol.,* **1,** 107 (1946); *ibid.,* **2,** 215 (1946).
9. Justi, E., and co-workers, *Jahrb. Akad. Wiss. Lit., Mainz* (1955); *ibid.,* 1956, No. 1. See also: H. Spengler, *Angen. Chem.,* **68,** 689 (1956).
10. Bacon, F. T., *Beama J.,* **61,** 6 (1954).
11. Kordesch, K., and Marko, A., *Oesterr. Chem. Ztg.,* **52,** 125 (1951).
12. Kordesch, K., and Martinola, F., *Monatsh. Chemie,* **84,** 1, 39 (1953).
13. Hunger, H., and Marko, A., 5th World Power Conference, Vienna 1956, No. 275 (paper K/11), H. Hunger, Dissertation, University of Vienna, 1954.
14. Marko, A., and Kordesch, K., U. S. Patents 2,615,932 and 2,669,598.
15. Witherspoon, R. R., Urbach, H. B., Yeager, E., and Hovorka, F., Tech. Report 4, Western Reserve University, ONR Cont. Nonr 581 (00), 1954.
16. Kordesch, K., and Marko, A., *Microchemica Acta,* 36/37, 420 (1951), K. Kordesch and E. M. King, BuShips Cont. Nobs 72374 (1958).
17. Vielstich, Wolf, *Z. physik., Chem.,* **15,** 409 (1958).
18. Hunger, H., Proceedings, Twelfth Annual Battery Research and Development Conf. U. S. A. S. R & D Lab., 1958.
19. Kordesch, K., Electrochemical Society Meeting, October, 1956, paper, Abstract No. 27. U. S. Patent 2,662,211.

3. Catalysis of Fuel-Cell Electrode Reactions

G. J. Young and R. B. Rozelle

Catalysis Laboratory
Alfred University
Alfred, New York

Research on fuel cells over the past few years has resulted in the development of commercial prototype fuel gas cells operating on such gases as hydrogen, carbon monoxide, and hydrocarbons. Several considerations[1, 2, 3] dictated the choice of this type of fuel cell (which includes all cells operating directly on fuel gases) for initial development. Depending on projected applications and power requirements, fuel gas cells have been designed to operate at low and medium temperatures using aqueous electrolytes[4, 5, 6] and at higher temperatures using molten salt electrolytes.[3, 7]

Fuel gas cells, particularly those operating at lower temperatures, may be subject to an irreversible free energy process resulting from the interaction of the reactant gases with the electrode surfaces.[3, 8] The reactant gases are chemisorbed by the electrode catalyst (or the electrode surface, which may act in a similar manner), and the reaction established is between the chemisorbed species and the electrolyte. The potential (free energy) developed by the cell, therefore, will depend on the equilibrium conditions of the chemisorbed species; and has been shown[8] to be approximately proportional to the heat of chemisorption. Thus, the catalyst surface can play a dual role in fuel cell electrode reactions: it can enhance the rate of reaction if chemical kinetics is rate-controlling—thus playing its usual role as a catalyst—and secondly, it can influence the potential of the cell by minimizing the free energy loss due to chemisorption.

While it is evident that the proper selection of catalysts in the design of fuel cell electrodes is essential for optimum performance, very little systematic work in this area has been published. Our present understanding of catalysis and surface physics, while far from complete, is nevertheless sufficiently comprehensive to enable a general explanation of fuel cell catalysts to be given. This chapter is concerned with a discussion of the activity

23

of a variety of catalysts for both the fuel electrode and oxygen (air) electrode, thus providing a guide to the selection of catalysts for specific cell reactions.

FUEL ELECTRODE

The role of the catalyst at the anode in a fuel gas cell is twofold: (1) it must rapidly chemisorb the fuel gas in such a manner as to make it more susceptible to oxidation by the active species of the electrolyte, and at the same time (2) it should act to minimize the free energy loss due to chemisorption. Thus, the criterion for an active catalyst is generally weak, but rapid chemisorption of the fuel gas. In the selection of a catalyst these conditions must be met; and moreover, the catalyst surface must preferentially chemisorb the fuel gas species over the reaction products in order to preclude self-poisoning.

Hydrogen

The chemisorption of hydrogen, particularly on metal surfaces, has been studied more extensively than that of other fuel gases. At normal temperatures, chemisorption of the type required for high catalytic activity is dissociative, and involves the formation of a partially covalent surface bond between hydrogen atoms and the d electrons of the metal. Thus, one general requirement for high catalytic activity of a metal in simple gas reactions of hydrogen is that it possess d band vacancies. This limits the active metal catalysts to the transition elements; however, not all transition metals are active catalysts, even though they chemisorb hydrogen. The early members of the transition series, which have vacancies in both the first and second d sub-bands, chemisorb hydrogen strongly, but they are in general not as active catalysts in hydrogen reactions as the later members of the three transition series, which have vacancies only in the second d sub-band. These metals exhibit the lowest heats of chemisorption at the surface coverages involved in heterogeneous reactions and are recognized as highly active catalysts for hydrogen reactions. Thus, it would appear that the most active metals for fuel cell electrode reactions where hydrogen is the fuel gas should be selected from those transition metals having d-band vacancies only in the second sub-band, e.g., the Group VIII metals.

Confirmation of the views stated above is given in Figure 3-1, where the open-circuit potentials for the anode half-cell with hydrogen are plotted as a function of the approximate number of d-band vacancies of the $5d$ transition metals and their alloys when used as catalysts at the hydrogen electrode (these potentials are negative relative to the normal hydrogen electrode).

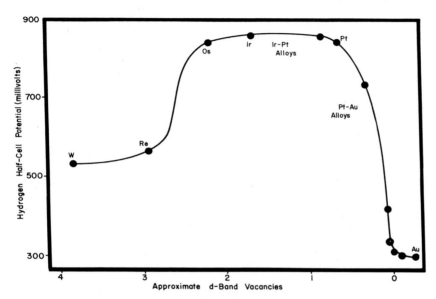

Figure 3-1. Hydrogen half-cell potentials as a function of d-band vacancies of the catalyst.

In general the catalytic activities of the metals parallel their open-circuit potentials, i.e., a small free energy loss due to chemisorption generally implies a high catalytic activity. Tungsten and rhenium both have relatively low open-circuit potentials and high heats of chemisortion. The alloys of platinum-iridium appear to exhibit a maximum in catalytic activity at about one d-band vacancy. As the vacancies in the d-band of platinum are filled by the s electrons of gold upon alloying, the fuel cell potential decreases sharply until the 60 per cent Au 40 per cent Pt alloy is reached, after which the potential appears to remain relatively constant.

These data and those in Table 3-1 were obtained with a low-temperature fuel cell ($27°C$) employing an aqueous sodium hydroxide electrolyte. The electrodes were constructed of porous carbon and impregnated with the various metal and alloy catalysts. The metal crystallites deposited in the porous carbon were approximately $100Å$ in diameter and covered about 10 per cent of the carbon surface. Traces of oxygen were flushed from the components of the cell and the metal catalysts were carefully reduced with hydrogen *in situ* before immersion in the electrolyte. The fuel electrode half-cell reactions appear to be reversible with respect to the chemisorbed species, as indicated by a number of independent experiments.[8] Open-

FUEL CELLS

TABLE 3-1. OPEN-CIRCUIT HYDROGEN HALF-CELL POTENTIALS FOR GROUP VIII AND Ib METAL CATALYSTS

Fe 575	Co 745	Ni 830	Cu 385
Ru 870	Rh 850	Pd 836	Ag 380
Os 859	Ir 850	Pt 845	Au 305

circuit potentials corresponded to current densities less than 10^{-16} amp/cm^2 and were measured against a standard saturated calomel electrode.

Table 3-1 lists the open-circuit, hydrogen half-cell potentials for the Group VIII transition metals and the neighboring Ib metals. The same trend in catalytic activity is observed in the three transition series, the potential reaching a maximum between the last two transition metals and falling sharply for the following Ib metal. The irreversible free energy loss in chemisorption is larger for the Group VIII metals of the 1st series (Fe, Co, Ni) than for the metals in the second and third series. These metals are easily oxidized in the presence of the electrolyte, and potentials due to the metal-metal ion couple are frequently encountered, especially under current drain. Also, the metals of the first series are more susceptible to poisoning by impurity gases such as sulfur compounds. From several considerations platinum and palladium are probably the best catalysts for hydrogen electrodes in fuel cells. Although a maximum in activity is obtained with alloys of certain of these metals, the slight increase in potential over the pure metals would probably not justify the difficulties of alloying in commercial practice.

The results given in Table 3-1 for a low-temperature fuel cell using aqueous hydroxide electrolyte, in general, are paralleled by high-temperature cells employing molten salt electrolytes, although the free energy loss on chemisorption decreases with increasing temperature and consequently is of less importance. For example, palladium and platinum catalysts give higher open-circuit potentials with hydrogen as a fuel gas than does nickel, iron, etc., in molten salt electrolytes in the 200 to 300°C range. At relatively high temperatures (*ca.* 500 to 800°C) the nature of the hydrogen chemisorption changes for several of the Group VIII metals. Quite probably, hydrogen forms $d-s-p$ hybrid bonds with the metal. Indeed, in some cases the catalyst can be poisoned for use in low-temperature cells by being heated to a high temperature and then cooled in hydrogen. Presumably, this leaves chemisorbed on the surface the more strongly hybrid-bonded hydrogen which is not active in the electrode reaction at low temperatures. However, the activity of the catalyst can be restored by heating and cooling in helium.

It is seen, from the data in Table 3-1, that the Ib metals chemisorb hydrogen and show limited activities as electrode catalysts. The activity of these metals possibly can be attributed to d–s electron promotion, such promotion accompanying chemisorption. The energies required for d–s promotion in the metal surface layer are probably less than those obtained from spectroscopic data and do not necessarily fall in the same order as indicated by the half-cell potentials.

Acetylene and Ethylene

The catalytic activites of the Group VIII and Ib metals in the oxidation of ethylene and acetylene in a fuel cell appear to be similar to their activities with hydrogen. These reaction systems, however, are fundamentally more complex than those of the hydrogen cell. The reactions that occur at the anode are complicated by a number of factors, among which is the nature of the chemisorbed complex, since either carbon-carbon or carbon-hydrogen bonds may be broken in chemisorption and oxidation. Jenkins and Rideal[9] report from exchange experiments that carbon-hydrogen bonds are broken on chemisorption of ethylene, and the surface complex has a composition of about C_1H_1. More recent evidence from infrared spectra,[10] however, indicates that the mode of chemisorption is dependent on the type of surface present, ethylene sorbing associatively on a hydrogen-covered surface at 35°C. Since the catalysts were reduced *in situ* with hydrogen, this corresponds to conditions present at the start of the experiments. Acetylene chemisorption on a supported Ni surface produces ethyl groups.[10] This implies that a surface carbide is formed. However, the absence of any oxygenated organic compounds in either the electrolyte or exit gas stream (when the cell is operated under current drain) and the copious deposition of carbon at the anode indicate that the principal reaction is:

$$CH{\equiv}CH + 2OH^- = 2C + 2H_2O + 2e^-$$

The fuel cell employed for studies on ethylene and acetylene was similar to the cell used for hydrogen, except that the electrolyte was a 40 per cent aqueous solution of K_2CO_3. The gas pressures were slightly above atmospheric and the operating temperature was 27°C. The cathode process is a reaction between the chemisorbed oxygen complex and the hydroxyl ion of the electrolyte (pH 12.3). The oxygen half-cell is independent of the

TABLE 3-2

| Metal | Half-Cell Potential (millivolts) | |
	Ethylene	Acetylene
Fe	780	790
Co	675	715
Ni	605	536
Cu	302	475
Ru	362	438
Rh	365	488
Pd	265	465
Ag	095	294
W	405	460
Os	402	413
Ir	405	450
Pt	420	570
Au	060	185

concentration of $CO_3^=$ but its potential follows the Nernst equation for the change in concentration of the hydroxyl ion when this ion is added. The anode reaction probably also involves the hydroxyl ion.

The products of the reactions at the fuel electrode have not been fully determined, but first analyses indicate the presence of aldehydes, ketones, and CO_2 in ethylene oxidation.

The most active catalysts among the metals studied are the Group VIII metals of the first transition series along with palladium and iridium, as illustrated in Table 3-2.

The maximum in catalytic activity appears at a different place in each transition series. Silver and gold in the Group Ib metals, although possessing some activity, are poor catalysts. The activity of copper is comparable with the less active of the Group VIII metals.

The catalytic activities of the metals investigated for ethylene and acetylene oxidation are sensitive to the state of the catalyst surface. This is especially the case for the metals of the second and third transition series. If, after reduction, these metals are exposed to low partial pressures of oxygen, their activities are decreased considerably. The members of the first transition series also are susceptible to oxygen poisoning; however, such poisoning may lead to the establishment of a metal-metal ion oxidation potential; hence, the potential would no longer be valid for the oxidation of a fuel. The most active catalysts are produced by *in situ* reductions where the surface, after reduction, is not exposed to the atmosphere but remains constantly under hydrogen until the electrode-electrolyte contact is made.

As in the case of hydrogen, a low heat of chemisorption in either ethylene or acetylene will minimize the irreversible free energy loss at the fuel electrode and, therefore, produce a higher potential in the fuel cell. Probably the most influential factors on the heat of chemisorption of ethylene and acetylene are (1) a geometric factor, i.e., interatomic distances in the catalyst lattice, and (2) an electronic factor. The most favorable interatomic distance for ethylene hydrogenation, according to Beeck,[11] is 3.75Å as observed in catalyst activity in ethylene hydrogenation reactions. Since the crystal planes exposed in the metals in this investigation are not known, no prediction can be made from these results. Probably the more important factor is the electronic character of the catalyst, since only transition metals or near transition metals catalyze these reactions.

Carbon Monoxide

The fuel cell employed for carbon monoxide was the same as for ethylene and acetylene, the electrolyte being a 40 per cent aqueous K_2CO_3 solution and the operating temperature 27°C.

The catalytic activities of the metal catalysts investigated in the anodic oxidation of carbon monoxide are given in Table 3-3. The Group VIII

TABLE 3-3. HALF-CELL POTENTIALS (MILLIVOLTS) FOR CARBON MONOXIDE

—	—	W 462
—	—	Re 469
Fe —	Ru 475	Os 520
Co 440	Rh 540	Ir 510
Ni 495	Pd 570	Pt 545
Cu 190	Ag 225	Au 150

metals of the second and third transition series produce the higher half-cell potentials. For the third transition series, there is an increase in potential from the Group VI metal, tungsten, to the Group VIII metals. The potential then decreases to gold. The activities of all the Ib metals are low. This would indicate the necessity of vacancies in the d band of the metal for a high activity.

The mechanism at the anode is probably similar to that of hydrogen in that a low heat of carbon monoxide chemisorption, at coverages where the reaction takes place, will minimize the free energy loss in the half cell. The chemisorption of carbon monoxide may take place by a number of different mechanisms, depending on the metal surface employed. On certain metals, such as supported platinum, it chemisorbs principally with a one-site attachment[10] forming a surface layer similar in structure to the metal carbonyls, i.e., M=C=O or M—C≡O. The second mode of chemisorption is a two-site sorption, the carbon monoxide complexes covering two surface sites as indicated in part (A) of the following diagram:

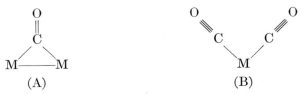

(A)   (B)

Two-site chemisorption takes place in this manner on palladium.[10] Another type of chemisorption that has been observed is a single site-two CO complex as in (B). This complex has been observed on rhodium samples.[10] All the transition metals investigated chemisorb carbon monoxide.

The decreased activity in the first transition series may be due to the ease of formation of the metal carbonyls. A more strongly bound carbon monoxide species would increase the irreversible free energy loss on sorption, and hence would decrease the half-cell potential. Again, these metals are readily oxidized by the electrolyte. Cell characteristics measured under current drain indicated that oxidation of the metal was occurring.

OXYGEN (AIR) ELECTRODE

The general requirements of a catalyst at the oxygen electrode of a fuel gas cell are similar to those of the fuel electrode, except that negative ion formation is the process under consideration. In cells employing aqueous hydroxide or aqueous carbonate electrolytes, the oxygen must chemisorb in such a manner as to lead to the rapid formation of peroxide and hydroxyl ions in the presence of water. A further role of the catalyst in this case is to aid in the decomposition of the peroxide ion.

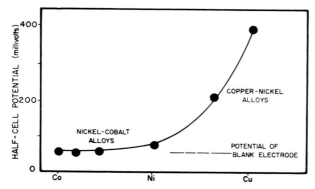

Figure 3-2. Oxygen half-cell potentials for Co-Ni-Cu alloys.

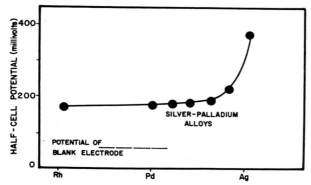

Figure 3-3. Oxygen half-cell potentials for Rh-Pd-Ag alloys.

The open-circuit single-electrode potentials of the oxygen electrode in an aqueous hydroxide electrolyte (pH 14) were determined for the Groups VIII and Ib metal oxides and oxides of their alloys as catalysts (with many of the metals this may be only a surface oxide). The later members of each series of the Group VIII metal oxides gave potentials only slightly greater than the unactivated carbon electrodes (Figures 3-2 and 3-3). The oxides formed by alloying the Group VIII metals with the Ib metals immediately following in a transition series produced only a small change in potential until appreciable amounts of the Ib metal were present. The potential then increased rapidly, as illustrated in the figures.

In fuel cell reactions proceeding by negative ion formation, which may be the rate-determining step, the work function of the catalyst surface is a major factor in determining the activity. The requirements of a small free energy loss due to chemisorption and of a weak, rapid chemisorption of the oxygen species would be met most readily by catalysts with a relatively low work function. The work functions for the Ib metal oxides supposedly are less than for the Group VIII oxides. Our data for the single-electrode potentials using copper-nickel alloys are similar to the results obtained by Dowden and Reynolds[12] with these alloys in the decomposition of hydrogen peroxide. This occurs by a negative ion mechanism,[13] and these investigators found that the activity of the alloys (presumably with an oxide layer) increased in the same manner as the half-cell potential in Figure 3-2 as progressively more copper was included in the alloy.

The results obtained for the oxygen electrode, where a low work function is one primary requisite of a high potential (weak chemisorption), may be contrasted with the data for the hydrogen electrode where a high catalytic activity probably involves a partial covalency of the fuel gas with the d electrons of the metal catalyst. For the hydrogen electrode, nickel (and other Group VIII metals) was an active catalyst, and subsequent alloying with copper, by filling the d-band vacancies of the nickel, decreased the activity. At the oxygen electrode alloying with the Ib metal increased the activity.

The most active catalysts, among those investigated, for the electrode reactions of the oxygen half-cell in aqueous hydroxide electrolytes are the oxides of the Group Ib metals: copper, silver and gold. Copper and silver oxides are known to be active catalysts in oxidation reactions and their presence presumably also promotes decomposition of peroxide ions formed under current drain. Gold films, however, have been reported to be inert toward the chemisorption of oxygen up to 0°C.[14] Possibly O_2^- ions are formed on the gold surface as an intermediate step in the reduction of oxygen. Such a species, if present in small amounts, might not be detected in chemisorption experiments since it would be readily removed from the surface on outgassing. The activities of the Ib metal oxides are in the order: copper > silver > gold.

The activity of some of the oxides as catalysts at the oxygen electrode may be varied considerably by the introduction of a defect structure. It is well known that heterogeneous reactions proceeding by negative ion formation can be profoundly altered by the defect state of the catalyst surface.

References

1. Liebhafsky, H. A., and Douglas, D. L., Paper 59-A-22 published by the American Society of Mechanical Engineering, 1959.
2. Young, G. J., and Rozelle, R. B., *J. Chem. Ed.* **36,** 68 (1959).
3. Broers, G. H. J., "High Temperature Galvanic Fuel Cells," Ph.D. Thesis, University of Amsterdam, 1958.

4. Evans, G. E., Proceedings of the Twelfth Annual Battery Conference, p. 4, 1958.

5. Bacon, F. T., *Beama J.*, **61,** 6 (1954).

6. Bacon, F. T., British Patent 677,298 (1952).

7. Gorin, E., and Recht, H. L., Paper 58-A-200 published by the American Society of Mechanical Engineering, 1958.

8. Rozelle, R. B., and Young, G. J., *J. Phys. Chem.*, in press.

9. Jenkins and Rideal, *J. Chem. Soc.*, **1955,** 2490.

10. Eischens, R. P., and Pliskin, W. A., "Advances in Catalysis," Vol. X, New York, Academic Press Inc., 1958.

11. Beeck, O., *Rev. Mod. Phys.*, **17,** 61 (1945).

12. Dowden, D. A., and Reynolds, P., *Discussions Faraday Soc.*, **8,** 184 (1950).

13. Haber, F., and Weiss, J., *Proc. Roy. Soc.*, **A147,** 332 (1934).

14. Trapnell, B. M. W., *Proc. Roy. Soc.* **A218,** 566 (1953).

4. Electrode Kinetics of Low-Temperature Hydrogen-Oxygen Fuel Cells

L. G. AUSTIN

Fuel Technology Department
The Pennsylvania State University
University Park, Pennsylvania

In a short chapter such as this, it is impossible to do more than briefly summarize and explain some of the fundamental equations of electrode kinetics. It is believed, however, that there is a need for such a presentation since many of the workers interested in the field of fuel cells will not be familiar with the terms and concepts involved. The subject is treated with respect to the well known[1] low-temperature hydrogen-oxygen fuel cell employing porous conducting electrodes.

Basic Formulas

The following thermodynamic formulas form the basis of the more specific ones derived later and are presented for convenience. In any process

$$aA + bB + \cdots \rightleftharpoons mM + nN + \cdots$$

the change in free energy per mole of reaction from left to right is given by

$$\Delta G = -RT \ln K_p + RT \ln \frac{(M)^m (N)^n}{(A)^a (B)^b} \cdots \tag{1}$$

a, b, m, n are the number of molecules involved, $(A), (B), (M), (N)$ are the activities of the reactants and products and K_p is the equilibrium constant of the reaction.

For some arbitrary definition of a standard state where the activities are unity

$$\Delta G_0 = -RT \ln K_p \tag{2}$$

where ΔG_0 is known as the standard state free energy change. For a substance going from one activity, a_1, to another a_2, $K_p = 1$, and

$$\Delta G = RT \ln a_2/a_1 \qquad a_2 = a_1 e^{\frac{\Delta G}{RT}} \tag{3}$$

The rate of an activated chemical reaction in one direction is given by

$$v_1 = k_1(A)_1{}^a(B)_1{}^b \; (\quad) \cdots (\quad) e^{-\Delta G_0*/RT} \tag{4}$$

where v_1 is the rate of reaction, $(A)_1$, $(B)_1$ are the activities of reactant at the reaction condition, ΔG_0* is the free energy of activation at the standard state used to define the activities and K_1 is a constant for the reaction.

The electrical potential, E, involved for a change of free energy ΔG is given by

$$\Delta G = -nFE \tag{5}$$

where F is the Faraday and n is the number of electrons involved in the reaction. A consistent system of units must be used.

Open-Circuit Potentials

Hydraulic Analogy. At open circuit, when no current is drawn from the cell, the potential obtained from the cell is equal to the corresponding free energy change in transporting reactant to product under these ideal reversible conditions. Figure 4-1 shows a hydraulic analogy of a fuel cell at open circuit. Since it is impossible to measure the potential of a single electrode, it is necessary to have two electrodes, represented by the two U-tubes shown in the figure. The difference in levels of the liquid in each arm of a U-tube (e.g., h_1) represents the free energy change between the reactant and the product for a half-cell. For a fuel cell in which reactant is supplied continuously to each electrode and product removed continuously, the hydraulic analogy requires infinite reservoirs at the liquid levels; one of these is shown at A for illustration.

It is impossible to measure the voltage corresponding to h_1, but if the right-hand U-tube is considered as a reversible standard state hydrogen half-cell, h_2 is arbitrarily taken as zero, and Δ_p corresponds to the half-cell potential (with respect to the standard hydrogen half-cell) of the left-hand electrode. With valve V closed, that is, no flow through the system, $\Delta_p = h_1$, and the open-circuit potential, E_r (infinite external resistance is comparable to the valve being closed) is equivalent to ΔG. It is clear from the above that the potential change *through* the electrode-electrolyte surface is zero at zero current drain; the potential drop, Δ_p, exists *across* the

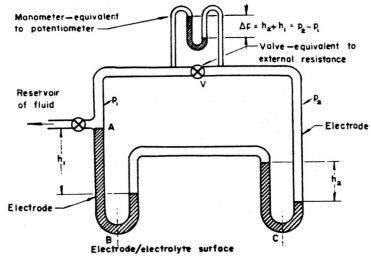

Figure 4-1. Hydraulic analogy of a hydrogen-oxygen porous electrode fuel cell.

external electrode to electrolyte connection. In an electrode process at open circuit, at the instant of electrode immersion, ions pass into solution across the electrode-electrolyte interface. The charge remaining on the electrode produces an attracting electric field preventing further dissolution. These forces are equivalent to the p_1 (suction) and P_2 (pressure) in the analogy.

Hydrogen Half-cell with Catalyzed Porous Carbon Electrode and Alkaline Electrolyte

The half-cell reaction can be represented as

$$H_2 + 2 \text{ active sites} \rightleftharpoons 2 \text{ [H] chemisorbed} \tag{6}$$

$$[H] + OH^- \rightleftharpoons H_2O + e + \text{active site} \tag{7}$$

At equilibrium, let the fraction of the active sites occupied by chemisorbed hydrogen be θ_e. The fraction of unoccupied sites is then $1 - \theta_e$ and the chemisorption equilibrium of reaction (6) can be represented[2] by

$$P(1 - \theta_e)^2 i = \theta_e^2 j \tag{8}$$

where i and j are rate constants and P is the pressure of hydrogen. Thus, from Equations (1) and (2), the free energy change on chemisorption is

$$(\Delta G)_C = (\Delta G_0)_C + RT \ln \theta/(1 - \theta)P^{\frac{1}{2}} \tag{9}$$

For reaction (7), the free energy change from the chemisorbed state to product, $(\Delta G)_{C-H_2O}$, is given by

$$(\Delta G)_{C-H_2O} = (\Delta G_0)_{C-H_2O} + RT \ln \frac{(H_2O)(1-\theta)}{(\theta)(OH')} \quad (10)$$

Substituting for $\theta/1 - \theta$ in Equation (9)

$$(\Delta G)_{C-H_2O} = (\Delta G_0)_{C-H_2O} + (\Delta G_0)_C - (\Delta G)_C + RT \ln \frac{(H_2O)}{(OH')P^{\frac{1}{2}}}$$

Now at equilibrium in the chemisorption process, Equation (1) shows that $(\Delta G)_C$ is zero; further $(\Delta G_0)_{C-H_2O} + (\Delta G_0)_C = (\Delta G_0)_{H_2-H_2O}$; therefore

$$(\Delta G)_{C-H_2O} = (\Delta G_0)_{H_2-H_2O} + RT \ln \frac{(H_2O)}{(OH')P^{\frac{1}{2}}} \quad (11)$$

where $(\Delta G_0)_{H_2-H_2O}$ is the over-all standard state free energy change from hydrogen to product. From Equation (5)

$$nFE_r = nFE_0 - RT \ln \frac{(H_2O)}{(OH')P^{\frac{1}{2}}} \quad (12)$$

Thus, at open circuit, the potential E_r would be expected to be independent of the chemisorption step and hence independent of the surface or catalyst used. Young and Rozelle[3, 4] have presented evidence to show that this is not true, and they ascribe the loss of potential on open circuit as being due to loss of free energy on chemisorption. This immediately raises the question as to why, when hydrogen is allowed to stand in contact with the catalyst surface the reversible potential is not observed.

A modification of the Freundlich adsorption isotherm suggested by Taylor and Halsey[5] gives θ as

$$\theta = (A_0 P)^{\frac{RT}{q_m}} \quad (13)$$

where a_0, q_m are constants. Clearly when $P = 1/a_0$, θ is 1, and hence $1/a_0$ represents a saturation pressure P_s, beyond which further increase in gas pressure (and hence gas free energy) produces no further free energy increase in the surface, and the system is irreversible. The loss of theoretical open circuit voltage is approximately

$$E_r - E_{\text{actual}} = \frac{-RT}{nF} \ln \frac{P}{P_s}, \quad P \leq P_s \quad (14)$$

Raising the temperature of the cell should bring the cell nearer to reversibility since P_s increases with temperature. Different catalyst surfaces presumably have different values for P_s .

Young and Rozelle[4] have correlated the loss of open-circuit potential with heats of chemisorption. This implies that the gas left in contact with the surface cannot reach a reversible equilibrium since the surface is saturated.

Loss of Potential During Current Flow

The polarization or loss of potential during current flow is obviously of prime importance in the design of fuel cells. To obtain good fuel efficiency the cell must be operated at a maximum internal voltage of about 20 to 30 per cent of the open-circuit voltage. If the current flowing per square centimeter of electrode area or per pound of cell is small, then the cell will be bulky and uneconomic. The theoretical analysis of polarization is an attempt to show which factors must be varied to obtain optimum conditions.

Consider the hydraulic analogy discussed previously. The transfer of ions across the electrode-electrolyte interface, being a chemical reaction, is activated, and the potential energy curve through the surface at open circuit can be visualized as in Figure 4-2. The energy is composed of the original chemical free energy and the electrical field energies, which counter-balance the chemical energy to give zero free energy change across the interface. Stated more precisely, the activities of the reactants and products at the surface change to bring the reaction into dynamic equilibrium. This produces a concentration of electrons in the electrode surface and a concentration of positive ions at the plane of closest approach in the electrolyte; the open-circuit potential is due to this double layer. Reducing the external resistance from infinity is comparable to opening valve V partially and allowing flow. Clearly a small flow will increase p_1 slightly and reduce p_2 ;

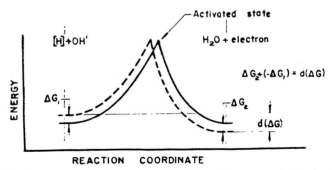

Figure 4-2. Representation of energy state of reaction across electrode-electrolyte interface.

Δ_P will decrease, and a pressure gradient is set up across B. In the electrical case this is equivalent to reducing the retaining electrical fields; consequently the energy curve on the left in Figure 4-2 rises and that on the right falls (see broken curves in Figure 4-2). The change in free energy through the surface on flow is clearly not available for outside potential, and E_r is reduced to E. The rest of the over-all free energy change of the reaction is carried through the external circuit by the electrons involved and the reaction can proceed only as fast as the external resistance will allow the current to flow, with Ohm's Law applying.

Let the change in free energy through the surface be $d(\Delta G)$. Then

$$\eta_a = E_r - E = \frac{-d(\Delta G)}{nF} \tag{15}$$

η_a is called the activation polarization at the given current flow. At short circuit, if there were no other resistances to flow present, then the drop of free energy through the surface would be the total free energy change and

$$\eta_a = \frac{-\Delta G}{nF} = E_r$$

where ΔG is the total free energy change of the reaction.

At open circuit a dynamic equilibrium exists across the interface,

$$[H] + OH^- \rightleftharpoons H_2O + e + \text{active site}$$

Let $(a_H)_e$ be the activity of the chemisorbed hydrogen at equilibrium, $(a_{OH})_e$ be that of OH', $(a_{H_2O})_e$ be that of water, and $(a_s)_e$ the activity of active sites. Then from Equation (4)

$$\text{forward reaction rate } v_{1e} = K_1(A_H)_e(A_{OH})_e e^{\frac{-\Delta G_{01}^*}{RT}}$$

$$\text{back reaction rate } v_{2e} = K_2(A_S)_e(A_{H_2O})_e e^{\frac{-\Delta G_{02}^*}{RT}}$$

The rate may be expressed as amps per square centimeter of active area, and at equilibrium $v_{1e} = v_{2e} = I'$. Under non-equilibrium conditions, from Equation (3)

$$(A_H)(A_{OH}) = (A_H)_e(A_{OH})_e e^{\frac{\Delta G_1}{RT}}$$

where ΔG_1 is the free energy change from equilibrium activities to those considered. A similar expression can be written for the back reaction with a free energy change of ΔG_2. Clearly the free energy changes represent the loss in free energy through the surface due to current flow and

$$-\Delta G_1 + \Delta G_2 = d(\Delta G) = -nF\eta_a$$

Let α be the fraction of η_a aiding the reaction from left to right. Then

$$\Delta G_1 = \alpha nF\eta_a$$

The new reaction rate from left to right is

$$
\begin{aligned}
v_1 &= K_1(A_H)(A_{OH})e^{\frac{-\Delta G_{01}^*}{RT}} \\
&= K_1(A_H)_e(A_{OH})_e e^{\frac{-\Delta G_{01}^*}{RT}} e^{\frac{\Delta G_1}{RT}} \\
&= I' \, e^{\frac{\alpha nF\eta_a}{RT}}
\end{aligned}
\tag{16}
$$

I' is the equilibrium current corresponding to rate in either direction at equilibrium. Similarly, $\Delta G_2 = -(1-\alpha)nF\eta_a$ where $1-\alpha$ is the fraction of η_a decreasing the reaction from right to left, and

$$v_2 = I'e^{\frac{-(1-\alpha)nF\eta_a}{RT}} \tag{17}$$

Thus the net current flow from left to right is

$$i' = I'\left(e^{\frac{\alpha nF\eta_a}{RT}} - e^{\frac{-(1-\alpha)nF\eta_a}{RT}}\right) \tag{18}$$

In general, part of the polarization in Equation (18) exists through the diffuse part of the double layer[6] extending from the plane of closest approach into the electrolyte. The structure of the double layer can be changed by the presence of the salts in the electrolyte, specific adsorption on the electrode surface and electrolyte concentration. Thus I' in Equation (18) is changed by these factors. It is easily shown[7] that I' may be represented as

$$I' = (I)_c e^{\frac{F\psi(\alpha n - z)}{RT}} \tag{19}$$

where ψ is the potential drop in the double layer and z is the number of electrons involved in transfer through the layer. $(I)_c$ is an equilibrium current which is more nearly characteristic of the reaction, while the term involving ψ can be used to explain the effects of modification of the double layer.[8] For the type of cell considered here, the composition of the electrolyte is usually dictated by other considerations and, if specific adsorption is avoided, the factor involving ψ is predetermined.

In Equation (18), the value of i' was derived per square centimeter of active site area. Normally, current is expressed per square centimeter of geometric electrode area and

$$i = (\text{constant}) \, N_s A_e i' \tag{20}$$

where N_s is the number of sites per unit effective area and A_e is the effective area per unit geometric electrode area. Then

$$
\begin{aligned}
i &= K N_s A_e I' \left(e^{\frac{\alpha n F \eta_a}{RT}} - e^{\frac{-(1-\alpha) n F \eta_a}{RT}} \right) \\
&= I \left(e^{\frac{\alpha n F \eta_a}{RT}} - e^{\frac{-(1-\alpha) n F \eta_a}{RT}} \right)
\end{aligned}
\tag{21}
$$

I is called the exchange current density as it is the equilibrium forward and reverse currents flowing at open circuit. This term is sometimes reserved for the equilibrium current for standard state conditions, I_0, but it is easy to convert from one to the other knowing the cell pressure and concentration (see Equation 24a).

Table 4-1 shows the values of i/I at various values of η_a; at room temperature and with $\alpha = \frac{1}{2}$, $n = 2(I\lambda/\lambda)$ it also gives values of i for various polarization for a range of I values. These results are shown graphically in Figure 4-3. Considering the results, it becomes apparent why some electrodes can be considered as reversible while others appear to be irreversible. For large exchange currents, the extrapolation of the curves to "zero" current (or the measurement of the open-circuit potential) will pass through the origin and give the theoretical reversible potential. Such electrodes are called reversible. On the other hand, for small exchange currents, the curve will appear to extrapolate to a finite polarization at "zero" current, due to the exponential nature of the function.

As η_a becomes larger (greater than about 50 millivolts) in Equation (21)

TABLE 4-1. RELATION BETWEEN i, I AND η_a GIVEN BY
EQUATION 22. (FOR $n = 2$, $\alpha = \frac{1}{2}$)

Activation polarization η_a mv	i/I	i ma cm^{-2}			
		I ma cm^{-2} = 10^{-6}	= 10^{-3}	= 1	= 10
10	.8	small	$.08 \times 10^{-2}$	.8	8
30	2.7		$.27 \times 10^{-2}$	2.7	27
50	6.7		$.67 \times 10^{-2}$	6.7	67
100	46	4.6×10^{-5}	4.6×10^{-2}	46	460
200	2100	2×10^{-3}	2	2100	
300	10^5	.1	100		
400	4.6×10^6	4.6			
500	2.2×10^8	220			

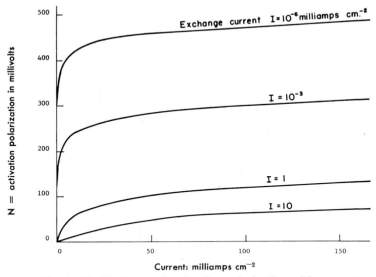

Figure 4-3. Variation of activation polarization with current.

(and if α does not alter in value) then the reverse reaction becomes negligible and

$$i = Ie^{\frac{\alpha n F \eta_a}{RT}} \tag{22}$$

or

$$\eta_a = \frac{2.3RT}{\alpha nF} \ln i - \frac{2.3RT}{\alpha nF} \ln I$$

$$= a + b \ln i$$

where

$$a = \frac{2.3RT}{\alpha nF} \ln \frac{i}{I}$$

$$\tag{23}$$

$$b = \frac{2.3RT}{\alpha nF}$$

This is known as the Tafel equation. It applies when the polarization is greater than about 50 to 100 millivolts. For a required current, the polarization is small if I is large. Neglecting double layer effect,

$$I = KN_sA_e e^{\frac{-\Delta G^*_{01}}{RT}} \quad \text{(term in equilibrium activities)} \quad (24)$$

To obtain low polarization, it is desirable to have as much effective surface per unit geometric area as possible. This is accomplished by having a system of small pores with a high surface roughness in contact with the electrolyte. Thus when using porous carbon electrodes it is necessary to "activate" the carbon by reaction with air or steam. This burns open pores which were closed and increases the surface roughness. Again, since the reaction takes place at an area of contact of gas, solid and liquid, saturation of the surface with electrolyte will greatly increase polarization.

The function of the catalyst impregnated on the surface is to decrease the activation energy ΔG^*_{01} of the reaction.

Increasing the temperature increases I, but it also reduces the other term in Equation (21). Normally the polarization is markedly decreased by an increase in temperature. The effect of the quantity of catalyst is governed by N_s. As the quantity is increased from zero the polarization is decreased, but a saturation state is reached when the surface is completely covered with the optimum quantity of catalyst.

Increasing the gas pressure on the cell increases the equilibrium activities and should thus decrease polarization. It is easily shown that Equation (24) can be written as

$$I = kN_sA_e(a_p)^{\alpha}(a_r)^{1-\alpha} e^{\frac{-\Delta G_0^*}{RT}} e^{\frac{\alpha\Delta G_0}{RT}} \quad (24a)$$

where a_p represents terms in bulk activities of products, a_r represents bulk activities of reactants and ΔG_0 is the standard state free energy change. Thus the effect of changes of concentrations of reactants upon I can be readily calculated if α is known.

Activation Polarization of Chemisorption

Equation (21) was derived specifically for the reaction

$$[\text{H}] + \text{OH}' \rightleftharpoons \text{H}_2\text{O} + e + \text{active site}$$

However, it is possible that the preceding chemisorption of hydrogen is slow during current flow. If this is true, the electrochemical reaction comes into balance with the chemisorption and an additional polarization is introduced, due to free energy changes on chemisorption. Considering the reaction,

$$\text{H}_2 + 2 \text{ active sites} \rightleftharpoons 2\text{H},$$

the activities may be represented as P, $(1 - \theta)^2$ and θ^2. In a similar manner to the derivation of Equation (21)

$$i = KN_sA_eP(1 - \theta_e)^2 e^{\frac{-\Delta G_0^*}{RT}} \left(e^{\frac{\alpha n F \eta_a}{RT}} - e^{\frac{-(1-\alpha)n F \eta_a}{RT}} \right)$$

$$= I \left(e^{\frac{\alpha n F \eta_a}{RT}} - e^{\frac{-(1-\alpha)n F \eta_a}{RT}} \right)$$

where the rate constant, value of activation energy, and exchange current are for the chemisorption process. When the cell is supplying current, θ must decrease to allow more chemisorption*. If θ is near 1, a small decrease in θ produce much extra chemisorption but virtually no change in the back reaction; therefore the polarization completely aids the reaction from left to right and $\alpha = 1$. Since $n = 2$, the slope b of the Tafel line under these circumstances is

$$b = \frac{2.303RT}{2F} \approx 0.03 \text{ volt, at room temperature}.$$

If the chemisorption is fast compared to the electrochemical step, the value of θ does not change much; α is about $\frac{1}{2}$, n is 1 and the slope of the Tafel equation is about 0.12 volt.[10] Thus the slope of the Tafel equation gives a means of determining whether the chemisorption step or the electrochemical step is predominantly rate-controlling. For chemisorption rate-controlling, the function of the catalyst is to lower the activation energy of chemisorption. Activation and chemisorption activation polarization are considered in more detail by Parsons.[11] The standard state free energy changes for the general case are shown in Figure 4-4.

Referring again to the results of Young and Rozelle,[3, 4] the assumption can be made that their "open circuit" potentials all correspond to some small fixed current i_0 which is related to the sensitivity limit of the potentiometric measurements. From Equations (22) and (24)

$$I = i_0 e^{\frac{-\alpha n F \eta_c}{RT}} = KN_sA_eP(a_s)_e e^{\frac{-\Delta G_{0f}^*}{RT}}$$

Now

$$P(a_s)_e = (a_H)_e e^{\frac{\Delta G_{0c}}{RT}}$$

* For many chemisorptions the rate of chemisorption follows a Zeldovich rate law in which the apparent activation energy of chemisorption, based on θ and $1 - \theta$ as activities, changes linearly with θ.[11] In this case large changes of rate can occur with only small changes in θ. This explains why α is constant over wide ranges of current flow. For this case θ and $1 - \theta$ cannot be used as activities in the equations developed in this chapter, which are quite general providing the correct values of activities are used.

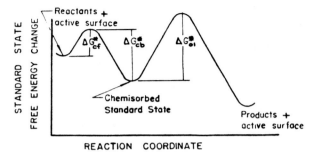

REACTION COORDINATE

Figure 4-4. Illustration of standard state free-energy changes during reaction.

where ΔG_{0c} is the standard state free energy of chemisorption. Defining a standard state immediately fixes the values of θ and $(1 - \theta)$ at the standard state θ_s, $(1 - \theta)_s$. The standard state free energy of chemisorption is then the free energy change in placing 1 mole of gas at standard state (1 atm) on the surface already having a fractional coverage of θ_s, the surface being so large that θ does not change during the transfer. Letting the activities be represented by θ terms

$$I = i_0 e^{\frac{-\alpha n F \eta_c}{RT}} = K N_s A_e (a_H)_e e^{\frac{-\Delta G^*_{cf}}{RT}} e^{\frac{\Delta G_{0c}}{RT}}$$

where

$$(a_H)_e \propto \theta_e \tag{25}$$

and

$$p(1 - \theta_e) = \theta_e e^{\frac{\Delta G_{0c}}{RT}}$$

When ΔG_{0c} has a large negative value (high exothermic heat of chemisorption) θ_e tends to 1, the variation of θ compared to $1 - \theta$ can be neglected and $(aH)_e$ can be assumed to be constant when ΔG_{0c} is varied. Since Young and Rozelle used the same type of carbon to prepare a number of electrodes each impregnated with a different catalyst, we may assume that variations in $K N_s A_e$ were small compared to variations in the exponential terms and

$$e^{\eta_c} \propto e^{\frac{\Delta G^*_{cf}}{RT}} e^{\frac{-\Delta G_{0c}}{RT}} \tag{26}$$

If chemisorption is the predominant rate-controlling factor the measured polarization is principally η_c. Thus from Equation (26) it may be predicted that if the activation energy of chemisorption is the same for different catalysts then

$$\eta \propto -\Delta G_{0c} \propto q \tag{27}$$

where q is the exothermic heat of chemisorption when θ tends to 1. This is the relation found experimentally by Young and Rozelle[4] for Pt, Ni, Fe and Cu catalysts and hydrogen fuel. It will be noted that this relation applies only for a number of restricting assumptions. The most stringent of these is that the activation energies of chemisorption are approximately equal for the different catalysts. Where the mechanism of chemisorption is the same, e.g., a covalent bond of hydrogen with the metallic d electrons in the case of transition metals, it does not appear unreasonable to expect that the activated complex of chemisorption is very similar for each material, even though the decay product, the chemisorbed gas, is widely different energetically from one metal to another. The relation of Equation (27) is certainly not general, and it would not even hold if potentials were compared between different base electrodes, as $N_s A_s$ would be widely different. It is also preferable to use polarizations at some known current rather than at "zero" current, since there is an element of doubt as to whether open-circuit potentials correspond to the same current for each catalyzed electrode.

Concentration Polarization

Concentration polarization is the loss of potential during current flow due to mass transport limitations in the cell. During current flow, the reactant has to be transported to the reaction site and energy is thus used in overcoming the resistance to flow which is always present.

Gas Transport Polarization. Gas transport through a porous carbon electrode is illustrated in Figure 4-5. If the reversible potential of the cell is for a pressure of P_1, then as the reaction proceeds and P_2 becomes less than P_1, the cell emf will fall. If the fall is η_c at a current of i

$$\eta_c nF = RT \ln \frac{P_1}{P_2} \tag{28}$$

Assuming the carbon has an effective diffusion coefficient D_{eff}, independent

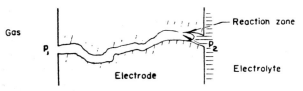

Figure 4-5. Illustration of gas transport process in a porous electrode.

of pressure[12] and that the electrode is in the form of a slab

$$\text{Rate} = D_{\text{eff}} \frac{(P_1 - P_2)}{\Delta L} \text{ per sq cm} \quad (29)$$

ΔL is the thickness of the electrode. Equation (29) may be expressed as

$$i = B(P_1 - P_2)$$

where B includes a conversion factor. Then

$$\eta_c = \frac{RT}{nF} \ln \frac{P_i B}{P_1 B - i}$$

Since the maximum value of $P_1 - P_2$ is P_1, BP_1, represents a limiting current, I_e, say, and

$$\eta_c = \frac{RT}{nF} \ln \frac{I_e}{I_e - i} \quad (30)$$

When i is small compared to I_e, η_c is linearly dependent on i; as i approaches I_e, polarization becomes very great. Thus it is desirable for I_e to be large. The thickness of the electrode cannot in practice be reduced beyond a certain limit. Due to the inhomogeneous nature of the pore system, reducing the thickness tends to produce either gas leakage from the surface or flooding of the pore system by the electrolyte. Thus it is desirable to have an electrode which has a high diffusion coefficient, high internal area or roughness factor, and which is as homogeneous in pore structure as possible. In operation, since P_2 has to be maintained sufficiently high to prevent electrolyte flooding, P_1 would have to be raised as concentration polarization becomes appreciable.

Electrolyte Concentration Polarization. In a manner similar to that above, the concentration polarization due to mass transfer of ions is

$$\eta_c = \frac{RT}{nF} \ln \frac{i_e}{i_e - i}$$

where the limiting current i_e is given by

$$i_e = \frac{D_i ZF a_i}{(1 - t_i)\delta} \quad (31)$$

D_i, a_i, t_i are, respectively, the diffusion coefficient, bulk activity and transport number of the ion and δ is the effective thickness of the diffusion layer adjacent to the electrode surface. This type of polarization is well described by Kortum and Bockris.[13]

The effect of concentration polarization can be introduced into Equation (21) by writing

$$\alpha_1 \eta_0 = \alpha \eta_a + \eta_c$$

where η_0 is the over-all polarization and η_c is the concentration polarization in the same direction as $\alpha \eta_a$. Considering just this direction,

$$i = I e^{\frac{\alpha n F \eta_a}{RT}}$$

$$= I e^{\frac{\alpha_1 n F \eta_0}{RT}} e^{\frac{-n F \eta_c}{RT}} \qquad (32)$$

$$= I \frac{C_r}{C_{r0}} e^{\frac{\alpha_1 n F \eta_0}{RT}}$$

where C_r is the effective activity and C_{r0} is the original bulk activity of the reactants. $C_r/C_{r0} = (I_e - i)/I_e$; thus i appears on both sides of Equation (32). The general form of the results is similar to that in Figure 4-6 in which I is taken as 10^{-3} ma/sq cm and I_e as 150 ma/sq cm. Also shown is the current voltage curve when the internal resistance of the cell is assumed

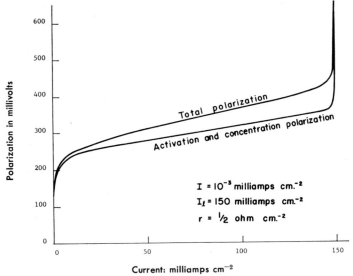

Figure 4-6. Illustration of polarization *vs.* current relations.

to be 0.5 ohm/sq cm of electrode. The introduction of concentration polarization in Equation (21) must be made for all the steps in the reaction which give appreciable concentration polarization.

Ohmic Resistance

In addition to the polarization already described an internal loss of potential, η_r, occurs due to the electrical resistance of the electrolyte. By Ohm's Law

$$\eta_r = ir$$

r is low for high concentration of ions in the electrolyte. It is of interest to note that if penetration of electrolyte into the pore system occurs, then the effective conductivity for ionic conduction is[14]

$$C_{\text{eff}} = \frac{\epsilon}{q} C \text{ free} \tag{33}$$

where ϵ is the porosity of the carbon and q is a tortuosity factor. For porous carbon electrode, ϵ is of the order of $1/3 \cdot q$ may be very high[15] but is often[16] about 2 to 3. Thus penetration of 1 mm will usually give as high an electrical resistance as abou 1 cm of the free electrolyte between the electrodes.

The Oxygen-Alkali Half-Cell

If the oxygen half-cell reaction were

$$\tfrac{1}{2}O_2 \rightleftharpoons [O], \qquad [O] + H_2O + 2e \rightleftharpoons 2OH'$$

then the standard state potential of a hydrogen fuel cell should be about 1.23 volts at room temperature. However, it has been shown[17, 18] that the half-cell reaction is

$$[O_2] + H_2O + 2e \rightleftharpoons HO_2' + OH'$$

Since the normal cell is not standard with respect to peroxide concentration, then open-circuit potential is usually not the voltage corresponding to the standard state of the above reaction. It is easily shown that if the peroxide ion is rapidly decomposed to its equilibrium value with respect to oxygen (in the electrode) and hydroxyl then the cell voltage would again be 1.23 volts. Even if peroxide decomposing catalysts are employed it appears that, at room temperatures, the decomposition is not sufficiently rapid for this equilibrium to be reached near the electrode surface and a loss of ideal potential occurs.[19] In practice the voltage is usually between 0.9 and 1.23 volts.

Conclusion

In studying the polarization type of fuel cells considered here, it is important to determine the contribution of each type of polarization to each half-cell. If such determinations are made, they will indicate what can be done to improve the performance of the cell. The various techniques for determining each polarization are described in the literature.[10, 13, 20] However, even if optimum conditions for minimum polarization are obtained, there are still many mechanical and technological difficulties to overcome in the construction of operating fuel cells.

References

1. Evans, G. E., Proceedings, Twelfth Annual Battery Research and Development Conference, U. S. Army Signal Research and Development Laboratory, 1958 Symposium on Fuel Cells.
2. Trapnell, B. M. W., "Chemisorption," p. 111, Butterworth's Scientific Publications, London (1955).
3. Young, G. J., and Rozelle, R. B., *J. Chem. Ed.*, **36**, 68 (1959).
4. Young, G. J., and Rozelle, R. B., *J. Phys. Chem.*, in press.
5. Halsey, G., and Taylor, H. S., *J. Chem. Phys.*, **15**, 624 (1947).
6. Frumkin, A. N., Bagotskii, V. S., Iofa, Z. A., and Kabanov, B. N., "Kinetics of Electrode Processes," p. 177, Moscow University Press, Moscow, 1952.
7. Berzius, T., and Delahay, P., *J. Am. Chem. Soc.*, **77**, 6448 (1955).
8. Frumkin, A. N., *Trans. Faraday Soc. (London)*, **55**, 156 (1959).
9. Rüetschi, P., *J. Electrochem. Soc.*, **106**, 819 (1959).
10. Potter, E. C., "Electrochemistry," p. 133, London, Cleaver-Hume Press Ltd., 1956.
11. Parsons, R., *Trans. Faraday Soc. (London)*, **54**, 1053 (1958).
12. Walker, P. L., Jr., Rusinko, F., and Austin, L. G., "Advances in Catalysis," Vol. XI, Chapter on Gas Reactions of Carbon, New York, Academic Press, Inc., 1959, in press.
13. Kortüm, G., and Bockris, J. O'M., "Textbook of Electrochemistry," p. 400, Vol. II, New York, Elsevier Publishing Co., 1951.
14. Carman, P. C., "Flow of Gases Through Porous Media," p. 46, New York, Academic Press Inc., 1956.
15. Hutcheon, J. M., Longstaff, B., and Warner, R. K., Preprints of Conference on Industrial Carbon and Graphite (London), 1957, "Flow of Gases Through Fine-Pore Graphite."
16. Wiggs, P. K. C., Preprints of Conference on Industrial Carbon and Graphite (London), 1957, "Gas Permeability and Pore Size Distribution."
17. Berl, W. G., *Trans. Electrochem. Soc.*, **83**, 253 (1943).
18. Witherspoon, R. R., Urbach, H., Yeager, E., and Hovorka, F., Technical Report No. 4, Electrochemistry Research Laboratory, Western Reserve University, 1954.
19. Kordesch, K., and Marko, A., *Osterr. Chem. Ztg.*, **52**, 125 (1951).
20. Broers, G. J. J., Ph.D. Thesis, University of Amsterdam, 1958.

5. The High-Pressure Hydrogen-Oxygen Fuel Cell

F. T. Bacon, M.A., A.M.I. Mech. E.

Marshalls Flying School, Ltd.
Cambridge, England

Introduction

The hydrogen-oxygen cell is particularly attractive, compared with other types of fuel cells, for a number of reasons. It has always appeared likely that a practical device could be developed to work at low or medium temperatures, and this raises the interesting possibility that it could be used as a kind of electrical storage battery, the two gases having been previously generated by the electrolysis of water, using power produced on a large scale.

When the author first became interested in fuel cells in 1932, a search of the available literature showed that the most promising results had in fact been obtained with this type of cell. The cell was first described by Sir William Grove in 1839,[1] and in 1889 particularly good results were recorded by the great chemist Ludwig Mond and his associate Charles Langer.[2] They achieved a current density of 6 amp/ft^2 (6.5 ma/cm^2) at 0.73 volt, using either oxygen or air; they also showed that the best results were obtained when the platinized platinum electrodes were kept substantially dry on the gas side. Further progress was prevented largely because of the high cost of the platinum electrodes.

Since World War II, a great deal of interesting work has been done in many countries on the hydrogen-oxygen cell, but this will not be discussed in detail here. Reference should be made however to the work of Davtyan[3] and Kordesch[4] and his associates.

Types of Cell Investigated

In 1938 a small cell similar to Grove's original gas battery was constructed and fair results obtained, but when activated nickel gauze electrodes were used in conjunction with an alkaline electrolyte of potassium hydroxide, the

51

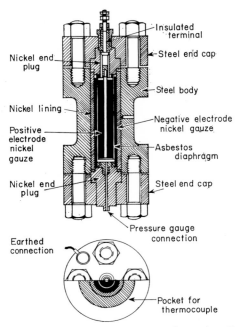

Figure 5-1. Apparatus for using coils of gauze as electrodes. Gas supply by initial electrolysis.

results were poor, even when the temperature was raised to the boiling point of the liquid.

It was then decided that the problem would have to be attacked essentially from an engineering point of view, and that operation under pressure could not be avoided if high current densities were to be obtained in conjunction with comparatively cheap materials, such as nickel. In 1939 a cell was designed which would withstand a pressure of 3000 psi and any reasonable temperature (Figure 5-1).

The electrolyte was a 27 per cent solution of potassium hydroxide and the cylindrical electrodes were of nickel gauze, activated by alternate oxidation in air and reduction in hydrogen. The electrolyte was separated from the electrodes by a diaphragm of asbestos cloth. Other metals, such as platinum, palladium, silver and copper were tried, but were discarded in favor of nickel, partly because of low cost and good corrosion resistance, but mainly because of its superior performance under current drain. It was found finally that a current density of 12.2 amp/ft^2 (13.1 ma/cm^2) of the external surface of the inner electrode could be maintained for 48 min. at about 0.89 volt, with a temperature of 100°C; many thicknesses of gauze and fairly high pressures were used to get these results. Curiously enough, there was no advantage in using temperatures higher than 100°C, and this was tentatively ascribed to the irreversible anodic oxidation of the oxygen electrode during the charging period.

The next step was to construct two cells, one acting as an electrolyzer for generating the two gases and the other as the current-producing cell (Figure 5-2). Gases produced in the electrolyzer were carried separately up into the cell in solution in the electrolyte, the liquid returning to the electrolyzer through separate pipes. Activated nickel gauze electrodes and asbestos diaphragms were again used, but this time in the form of flat discs.

The performance of this cell improved continuously with increasing temperatures and pressures up to 240°C and 1075 psi—the highest tried. The highest current density obtained at 240°C was 75 amp/ft^2 (81 ma/cm^2) at 0.65 volt with six gauze electrodes on each side of the cell. The current density appeared to be limited by the rate at which fresh gas could be carried up to each electrode in solution in the electrolyte. The materials and methods of construction employed proved to be reasonably satisfactory.

The Present Cell with Diffusion Electrodes

The performance of the cell was still not considered good enough for any practical application. Keeping in mind that high pressures inevitably lead to higher container weights than would be necessary for a fuel cell operating at atmospheric pressure, it was decided that a new apparatus should be built with gases confined to the backs of the porous nickel electrodes; this design has been employed with very little change ever since.

Construction details have frequently been described before,[5] but it is probably best to recapitulate them briefly at this time.

A single cell is illustrated diagrammatically in Figure 5-3. The electrodes are made of porous sintered nickel, and the main parts of the cell are of nickel-plated steel or pure nickel; the electrolyte is a strong potassium hydroxide solution, ranging between 37 and 50 per cent concentration. The normal operating conditions are 200°C and 300 to 600 psi. At the present time, a pressure of 400 psi is normally used. The porous nickel electrodes, which are about $\frac{1}{16}$-in. thick, have a pore size of about 30 microns or more, on the gas side, with a thin layer of much smaller pores on the liquid side. A small pressure difference is set up in the apparatus across each electrode, so that the liquid is expelled from the large pores on the gas side, but the gas cannot bubble through the smaller pores on the liquid side owing to the surface tension of the liquid. The interior of the 30-micron pores, which are

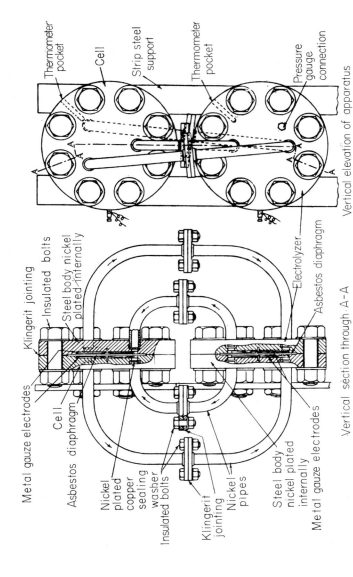

Figure 5-2. Apparatus using flat discs of gauze as electrodes. Gas supply from separate electrolyzer.

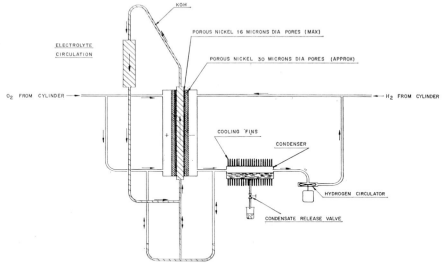

Figure 5-3. Apparatus embodying cell with porous diffusion electrodes.

wetted throughout with electrolyte, presents a large surface for absorption of gas. The oxygen electrodes are subjected to pre-oxidation treatment at a high temperature in air, and this protects them from corrosion by the high pressure oxygen and electrolyte. Lithium atoms are incorporated into the crystal lattice of the nickel oxide, thus converting the ordinary green nickel oxide, which is an insulator, into a black double oxide of nickel and lithium; this double oxide is a good semiconductor.

With this arrangement, the gases are supplied from cylinders in the normal way; other advantages over previous designs are: (1) the gas sides of the electrodes are coated with only a very thin layer of electrolyte, giving a very short diffusion path for the gases in solution before they reach the active surface of the electrodes, (2) the useful surface area of the electrodes is greatly increased, and (3) the asbestos diaphragm is eliminated.

Electrode Design

A good electrode design is of utmost importance, and several different designs have been tried. The largest electrodes made to date are 10-in. effective diameter, though this does not by any means represent any limit in size. They are sintered directly onto a flat circular perforated sheet of nickel or nickel-plated steel, about $\frac{1}{16}$-in. thick; this provides adequate strength and serves also to conduct away the current generated. Electrodes up to 5 in. diameter were made previously without a backing plate of solid metal, but it was considered unlikely that larger ones would be satisfactory without adequate support. Separators, in the form of narrow vertical strips of polytetrafluoroethylene (PTFE) have to be used with 10-in. diameter electrodes, to prevent internal short-circuits when the pressure difference is applied.

An alternative form of electrode has been employed comprising a bipolar structure with recesses machined on either side of a solid metal plate; each recess is filled with porous sintered nickel for hydrogen and oxygen electrodes, respectively. A thin dimpled perforated plate sintered into each recess provides a narrow space for conducting gas from ports in the rim to all parts of the porous metal. When bipolar electrodes of this type are assembled in series, with gaskets of insulating material between each, a series of cells is formed which does not require any external current connections except at each end of the battery. This electrode construction is attractive in many ways and makes a very compact battery. It has been abandoned temporarily however in favor of the simple unipolar design, owing largely to difficulties in manufacture.

The coarse pore layers of hydrogen electrodes are made from Grade B carbonyl nickel powder (average particle size 2 to 3 microns) mixed with about 20 per cent by weight of 100 to 240 mesh ammonium bicarbonate which acts as a spacing agent during sintering; it is pressed lightly in a rubber press, and then sintered for about $\frac{1}{2}$ hr at 850°C in a reducing atmosphere. The fine pore layer is then applied as a suspension of Grade A carbonyl nickel powder (average particle size 4 to 5 microns) in alcohol; this is sintered for $\frac{1}{2}$ hr at 800°C. Any leaks are repaired by further thin applications of Grade A nickel as before.

The coarse pore layers of oxygen electrodes are usually made from Grade D carbonyl nickel powder (average particle size 7 to 9 microns) mixed with 15 to 20 per cent of 100–240 mesh ammonium bicarbonate; it is pressed lightly and sintered for $\frac{1}{2}$ to 1 hr at 1000 to 1150°C in a reducing atmosphere. The fine pore layer is again of Grade A nickel, sintered for $\frac{1}{2}$ to 1 hr at 950 to 1000°C. Alternatively, the coarse pore layers of the oxygen electrodes may be made from a coarse nickel powder, about 200 to 250 mesh, without a spacing agent; but in this case a higher compressing pressure and a higher sintering temperature (1150°C as a minimum) are required to get a really strong compact.

Finally the oxygen electrodes are pre-oxidized after impregnation with a dilute solution of lithium hydroxide. Air is used for oxidation, and a satisfactory thickness of oxide is formed in $\frac{1}{4}$ to 1 hr at 700 to 800°C.

Hydrogen electrodes are activated by impregnation with a strong solution of nickel nitrate, followed by roasting in air at 400°C and, finally, reduction in hydrogen at about the same temperature. Work is proceeding on the activation of oxygen electrodes, but a standard treatment has not been arrived at as yet.

Typical microsections of hydrogen and oxygen electrodes are shown in Figures 5-4 and 5-5.

Prevention of Corrosion of Oxygen Electrodes

When porous nickel electrodes were first used, serious difficulty developed because of the gradual corrosion of oxygen electrodes; this caused a drop in output and eventually complete breakdown. This difficulty has been largely overcome by the pre-oxidation treatment described above. Samples of nickel pre-oxidized in air at about 800°C were found to be extremely resistant to corrosion when subsequently exposed to strong KOH solution and oxygen under conditions similar to those in the cell. But the green oxide layer produced during pre-oxidation acts as an electrical insulator, and electrodes protected in this way are useless in the cell. However, it was ascertained that lithium atoms incorporated into the crystal lattice of the nickel oxide produced a black double oxide of nickel and lithium, which is a good semiconductor,[6] and corrosion resistance is unimpaired or even enhanced. Using this technique, oxygen electrodes have been in operation for as long as 1500 hr at 200°C without failure, and with only a very slight reduction in performance. Specimens of pre-oxidized nickel have been exposed to oxygen under pressure and potassium hydroxide solution at 200°C for more than 10,000 hr without visible deterioration; and accelerated corrosion tests at higher temperatures have shown that considerable improvement should be possible. Before the pre-oxidation treatment had been introduced, experiments were made with various corrosion inhibitors dissolved in the electrolyte. Potassium silicate and potassium aluminate were particularly successful in preventing corrosion of oxygen electrodes, but they greatly reduced the performance of the cell. Thi was believed to have provided the explanation for the curious fact that no corrosion of oxygen electrodes was observed when the earlier cells were used with nickel gauze electrodes; all the earlier cells had diaphragms of asbestos cloth, and it was to be expected that the electrolyte would therefore become somewhat contaminated with potassium silicate or aluminate. It is interesting also that a small amount of copper, added to the KOH in the form of copper oxide, was effective as a corrosion inhibitor and that it resulted in the formation of a black oxide on the nickel.

FUEL CELLS

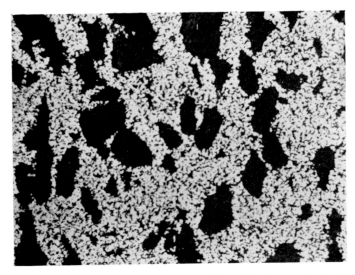

Figure 5-4. Microsection showing coarse pore side of hydrogen electrode (×150).

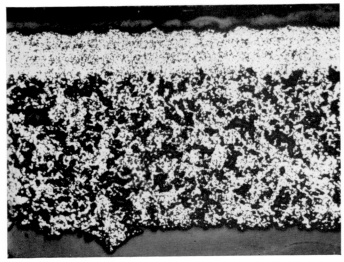

Figure 5-5. Microsection showing coarse and fine pore layers of oxygen electrode (×38).

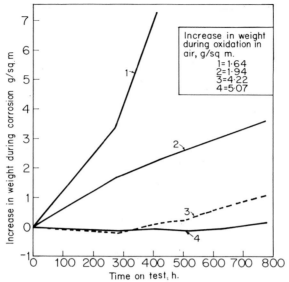

Figure 5-6. Corrosion of samples of nickel pre-oxidized in the presence of lithium hydroxide and exposed to 65 per cent KOH and oxygen at 300°C and 800 psi total pressure.

The results of some accelerated corrosion tests on samples of nickel pre-oxidized in the presence of lithium hydroxide, and exposed to 65 per cent KOH and oxygen at 300°C and 800 psi total pressure, are shown graphically in Figure 5-6. The samples were placed in oxidized nickel crucibles, which were set up in autoclaves; the samples were half in and half out of the KOH solution. The gas space was filled with oxygen under pressure, and temperature and pressure readings were recorded periodically. The autoclaves were opened at intervals and the samples washed in distilled water, dried and weighed; the extent of corrosion was indicated by the weight change. A fresh KOH solution was used in each run. These curves emphasize the importance of a sufficiently thick oxide layer, in order to obtain really good durability. It is estimated that an oxide layer about 3-microns thick can be obtained by coating the nickel with 2 g of lithium hydroxide per square meter of surface and oxidizing it in air at 800°C for 16 min.

Some results of tests at 200, 260 and 300°C are plotted in Figure 5-7. These samples are not exactly comparable owing to differences in the initial thickness of the oxide coating and in the conditions under which the corro-

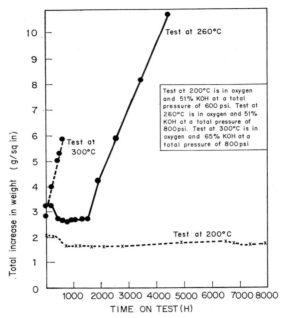

Figure 5-7. Curves showing the effect of temperature on corrosion rate.

sion tests were carried out. It is possible to say, however, that similar samples corrode at 200°C much more slowly than at 260°C. Also a further increase in corrosion rate is produced if the temperature is raised to 300°C. By pre-oxidizing the samples to produce an increase in weight of 5 g/m^2 instead of 2 to 3 g/m^2, the corrosion rate at 300°C was reduced considerably as shown in Figure 5-6. It seems reasonable to suppose that if the samples oxidized with lithium present to give an increase in weight of 5 g/m^2 were tested at 200°C, they would have a life many times longer than those already tested at this temperature (Figure 5-7). Even if it were to prove impossible to produce such a thick oxide layer on the oxygen electrode, a thinner layer of 2 g/m^2 will protect an electrode for more than 10,000 hr at 200°C.

Jointing Material

There must be at least one electrically insulated gasket per cell, and at present, using unipolar electrodes, four gaskets are required. Although many different materials have been used, none has been found that is superior in all respects to ordinary compressed asbestos fiber jointing, which is primarily composed of asbestos fiber and rubber (generally neoprene). This material has a number of disadvantages, the principal one being that the rubber content is gradually oxidized when exposed to high pressure oxygen; this eventually results in loss of strength and leakage to the atmosphere. However, runs of 800 hr have been achieved without failure, and runs greatly exceeding this should be possible with a superior design. Another disadvantage is that substances given off when the rubber decomposes on heating poison the hydrogen electrode and tend to reduce the output of the cell.

The best alternative to this type of jointing would appear to be PTFE loaded with asbestos fiber, or possibly with powdered glass. These materials however are only now in the process of development in England, and the metal surfaces would certainly have to be specially roughened to prevent slip. End pressure on the gaskets could no doubt be reduced by using a pressure cylinder or tank, in which the whole cell pack is contained under pressure. At present this line of development is not being pursued in England, owing to the extra complication involved.

Cell Performance

Cell performance improves with both temperature and pressure, but in order to attain a long life it will probably prove desirable to limit the working temperature to 200°C or slightly higher. The best performance obtained so far with a 10-in. diameter cell at 200°C and 400 psi is shown in Table 5-1, and plotted as a voltage-current density characteristic in Figure 5-8. The diameter of the sinter is somewhat less than 10 in.—approximately 9⅝ in.—but it is felt that it is more accurate to base the figures for current density on internal diameter of the body of the cell.

These figures were taken from one cell in a ten-cell battery, using 37 per cent KOH as the electrolyte. Both of these factors contribute to the rather low open-circuit voltage obtained. Under the above conditions of 0.68 volt and 440 amp/ft^2 (or 240 amp), the power output per unit of internal volume corresponds to 8.2 kw/ft^3. At the maximum output obtained so far, namely, 0.62 volt and 585 amp/ft^2 (or 320 amp) at 200°C and 600 psi, the power output per unit internal volume corresponds to 10 kw/ft^3.

TABLE 5-1

Current (amp/ft²)	0	10	50	100	200	300	440
Density (ma/cm²	0	11	54	107.6	215	323	473
Voltage, v	1.04	1.005	0.93	0.885	0.82	0.755	0.68

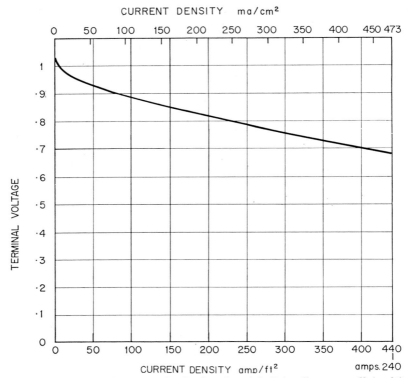

Figure 5-8. Best performance obtained so far with 10-in. diameter cell (multi-cell pack). (200°C; 400 psi; 37 per cent KOH).

The current efficiency, measured over a period of some hundreds of hours in a 5-in. diameter unit with two cells in series, is 98 per cent. This means that the energy efficiency, based on the free energy of the reaction, will approximate at any useful current density the voltage efficiency; e.g., at 0.9 volt and 200°C and 600 psi the energy efficiency will be $\frac{0.9}{1.20} \times 100 = 75$ per cent; at 0.8 volt it will be 66 per cent, and at 0.6 volt it will be 50 per cent.

When the cell is on load, the losses which appear in the form of heat, are primarily due to the irreversibility of the electrode reactions, or what may be called "activation polarization"; a smaller proportion of the losses are due to resistance and concentration polarization. On open-circuit, and at low current densities, there will also be a "lost current" due to diffusion of

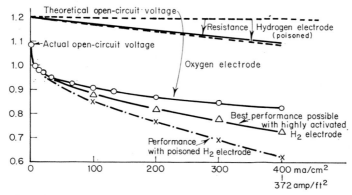

Figure 5-9. Performance of cell in terms of each electrode and resistance (40 per cent KOH; 200°C; 620 psi).

the two gases in solution through the electrolyte, followed by combination on the opposite electrode.

Figure 5-9 shows the relative proportions of polarization due to each electrode and to the electrolyte. Ordinary CAF jointing was used, so the hydrogen electrode was somewhat "poisoned." Assuming that activation of the hydrogen electrode can easily reduce polarization from this source to a negligible amount, while electrolyte resistance and oxygen electrode polarization are less easily improved, a curve can be drawn showing the best performance to be expected from a cell (see Figure 5-9). This shows that 223 amp/ft^2 (240 ma/cm^2) at 0.8 volt and 650 amp/ft^2 (700 ma/cm^2) at 0.6 volt can reasonably be expected at 200°C and 620 psi.

The experimental method has been improved by the measurement of purely resistive polarization in the cell circuit using a commutator technique in conjunction with a cathode ray oscilloscope, so that individual electrode performance can be studied precisely. This is particularly important in the case of the hydrogen electrode, where both resistance and activation polarization have the same linear dependence on the current. A reference electrode, in the form of a small resting (i.e., unloaded) hydrogen electrode of porous nickel, located in the electrolyte space, about halfway between the main hydrogen and oxygen electrodes, has made it possible to study the polarization in each electrode separately; a reference electrode of this kind is used fairly regularly in cell operation, even when the commutator technique is not employed. This has shown that polarization of the hydrogen electrode at 200°C, when plotted against current density, gives approximately a straight line; at lower temperatures, the behavior becomes loga-

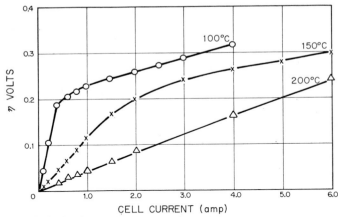

Figure 5-10. Polarization of hydrogen electrode at varying temperature in $5N$ KOH solution.

rithmic (see Figure 5-10). With the oxygen electrode, however, the behavior is logarithmic even up to the highest temperature tried. The shape of the curve which it gives at 200°C can be seen in Figure 5-9. The difference in shape of the polarization curves shown by the hydrogen and oxygen electrodes at 200°C can be explained by the fact that exchange current is much less in the latter case, or in other words, the oxygen electrode is much less reversible than the hydrogen electrode. In addition, the surface area of the oxygen electrode is much less than that of the hydrogen electrode. But even an oxygen electrode of large surface, made from Grade B nickel, will polarize more than a hydrogen electrode made from the same powder and with the same surface area. A large increase in surface area will be required to improve the performance of oxygen electrodes. This can probably best be obtained by some form of activation.

Since electrodes are made with a backing plate, it is possible to test hydrogen and oxygen electrodes as thin as $\frac{1}{32}$ in. The performance of these thin electrodes is within 20 per cent of that of previous electrodes which were $\frac{1}{8}$ to $\frac{5}{32}$ in. thick. With electrodes $\frac{1}{16}$ in. thick there does not appear to be any sacrifice in performance. A number of other hydrogen and oxygen electrodes of varying structures have been tested, but so far none has shown a striking improvement in performance when compared with standard types.

Effect of Cell Conditions on Performance

Pressure. The effect of temperature and pressure on the reversible voltage of the hydrogen-oxygen cell can be seen in Figure 5-11. Measurements

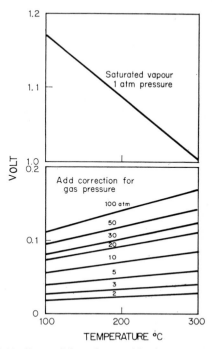

Figure 5-11. Reversible voltage of hydrogen-oxygen cell.

of electrode and cell performance at different gas pressures (the electrolyte vapor pressure having been measured, see Figure 5-12) show that small variations in pressure have only a slight effect. A tenfold change in gas pressure from 30 to 3 atm (441 to 44 psi) reduces cell performance approximately 50 per cent at normal operating voltages (see Figure 5-13). A theoretical analysis taken fairly recently shows that for a given power output, and assuming that the gases are both stored in high tensile steel cylinders at 3,000 psi, the over-all weight of the battery and storage cylinders would not be increased if the operating pressure were reduced from 600 to 300 psi; the efficiency however would be slightly reduced. This calculation allows for the "dead" fuel remaining in the cylinders when the battery is discharged, and also for reduction in weight of the battery itself.

Temperature. The maximum cell temperature is limited by the materials used in constructing it. Thus, PTFE is found to corrode relatively quickly at 250°C under cell conditions, where it comes in contact with porous nickel; and the nickel-lithium oxide of the oxygen electrode breaks

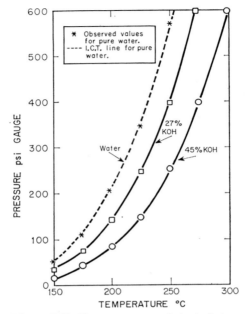

Figure 5-12. Vapor pressure of electrolytes.

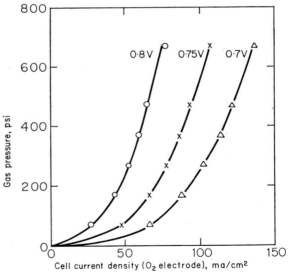

Figure 5-13. Variation of cell output with gas pressure for various voltages.

down fairly quickly at 300°C. Between 100 and 250°C the cell output at normal operating voltage increases rapidly with an increase in temperature, as the hydrogen electrode changes from logarithmic behavior at 100°C to linear behavior. After 200°C the output does not increase as rapidly as it does between 100 and 200°C. Taking 100°C as unit performance, that at 150°C is roughly 4, at 200°C it is 10, and at 250°C it is 15. The actual maximum power available (at a low efficiency) rises progressively with an increase in temperature, and is roughly doubled with each 50°C increase.

Electrolyte Concentration. Figure 5-14 shows the effect of vapor pressure of the electrolyte on the reversible voltage of the hydrogen-oxygen cell at 200°C, assuming that the total pressure is kept constant at 600 psi. It has been necessary to plot vapor pressure of the electrolyte, rather than the concentration, as the relationship between concentration and vapor pressure of very strong KOH solutions has not been measured, as far as is known.

It has been assumed that the disposable energy in the formation of water vapor at a constant pressure of 1 atm is 219.4 kilojoules/g formula weight,

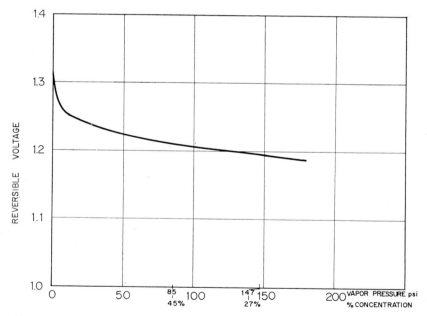

Figure 5-14. Relationship between reversible voltage and vapor pressure of the electrolyte (200°C; 600 psi; total pressure).

at 200°C. At other values of pressure the disposable energy is increased by an amount

$$0.5RT \ln_n \frac{(P_{H_2}^2 \cdot P_{O_2})}{(P_{H_2O}^2)},$$

the pressures being measured in atmospheres.

The theoretical voltage is obtained by dividing the disposable energy by $2F$, where F is the Faraday, 96,500 coulombs.

Increasing the concentration of the potassium hydroxide electrolyte to 35 per cent by weight increases the cell output progressively, but further increase from 35 to 45 per cent has less effect. Operation at concentrations higher than 45 per cent causes practical difficulties, e.g., the KOH electrolyte becomes solid on cooling. Long continuous operation of cells on load for periods of 50 to 100 hr has shown that very high concentrations of KOH cause a build-up of concentration polarization (absence of water in the oxygen electrode is the most probable cause), so that a concentration of approximately 35 per cent KOH seems to be the optimum at present. If it proves feasible to condense out twice the water formed from the hydrogen electrodes, and then return half of it to the oxygen electrodes in the form of steam mixed with oxygen, this difficulty should disappear and stronger concentrations could be contemplated.

The values obtained for specific conductivities of a range of electrolytes at various temperatures are shown in Figure 5-15. These were obtained by measuring cell resistance with two different inter-electrode distances using the commutator technique mentioned previously. They are only approximate. Results for 36 per cent KOH are particularly erratic, and measurement of conductivity using an a.c. bridge and high temperature conductivity cell should provide accurate results.

Values predicted by Fry[7] are also plotted; these were obtained by using the relationship between conductivity and viscosity and an estimated value of viscosity, and also values quoted by Bowen[8] for KOH (deduced from work by Kohlrausch in 1898). General agreement is observed.

The contribution of electrolyte resistances to cell operation will be approximately 0.25 ohm/cm^2 of apparent electrode surface for $\frac{1}{8}$ in. electrode spacing using electrodes of the types described. For a current density of 250 ma/cm^2, this would give a polarization of 0.0625 volt, i.e., a voltage drop corresponding to about 5 per cent of the total free energy available.

Shunt Currents in Multi-cell Packs. A six-cell pack of 5-in. diameter electrodes was constructed in 1954 and fair results were obtained.

Measurements of the shunt currents along the common electrolyte ports,

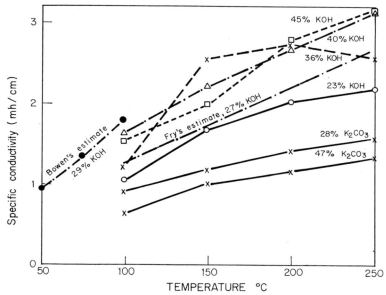

Figure 5-15. Variation of electrolyte conductivity with concentration and temperature.

and a theoretical treatment, suggest that the magnitude of shunt currents will depend largely on dimensions of the axial electrolyte ports through the pack.

If V = the open-circuit voltage of one cell

    n = the number of cells in the pack

    R = the resistance of one pair of axial ports in one cell, and

    r = the resistance of one pair of radial ports in one cell,

then the shunt current $= \dfrac{(n-1)V}{2r + (n-1)R}$

For large packs, where distribution of liquid may be important, it might be better to have a number of axial ports serving groups of cells, rather than one large port serving all the cells.

Use of Other Gases

It has often been suggested that a cell of this type could be used as a genuine fuel cell for generating power on a large scale, using hydrogen produced from coal by ordinary chemical methods, and oxygen from the air.

This is, of course, a very ambitious project and cannot honestly be envisaged at present, owing to the high cost of pure hydrogen produced in this way; pure oxygen is also expensive.

Nevertheless, it is obvious that the scope of the whole project could be greatly widened if it were found possible to use a liquid fuel that could be converted into a gas which is electrochemically active in the cell. It would thus become possible to compete on more equal terms with the internal combustion engine.

A number of experiments have been carried out using other gases, or mixtures of gases, and the conclusions can be summarized as follows:

(1) No other fuel gas, except hydrogen, has been found to be electrochemically active on a nickel electrode at temperatures which it would be practicable to use in cells of this type. Carbon monoxide, methane and methanol were tried and all were unsuccessful.

(2) Both carbon monoxide and carbon dioxide are soluble in caustic potash and would eventually result in carbonation of the electrolyte.

(3) Complete carbonation would seriously impair performance of the electrolyte, resulting in a reduction to one quarter of its normal performance. This is partly due to loss in oxygen electrode performance and partly to increased cell resistance.

(4) Hydrogen containing inert diluents, such as nitrogen or methane, can be used with a high volume percentage of inert gas, as long as provision is made for exhausting the residue; some hydrogen would no doubt be wasted in the exhaust, but the amount is not likely to be serious.

(5) Possibly because of its solubility in hot caustic potash solution, carbon monoxide does not poison the fuel electrode, but it may attack the nickel pipe-work conducting gas into the cell. No poisoning was observed with other gases used.

(6) Experiments using nitrogen-oxygen mixtures showed that air could be used in place of oxygen, as long as any left over nitrogen was continuously removed, and the carbon dioxide extracted before entry into the cell.

The above conclusions show that the presence of any gas, apart from hydrogen and oxygen, may create problems. On the other hand, small percentages of inert gases would do no harm to the cell, provided adequate means were worked out for exhausting such gases to the atmosphere from time to time, before they had built up to large proportions inside the electrodes. A small purification plant could no doubt be designed for continuously purifying a slightly carbonated electrolyte.

The additional polarization at the oxygen electrode caused by using air instead of pure oxygen can be seen in Figure 5-16; this also shows the effect of oxygen pressure on polarization. Figure 5-17 shows the effect of various

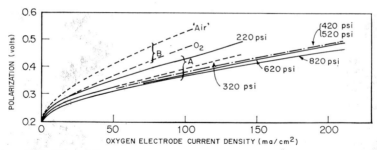

Figure 5-16. The effect of pressure on polarization at the oxygen electrode, (A) $5N$ KOH, 200°C; (B) $5N$ KOH, 200°C.

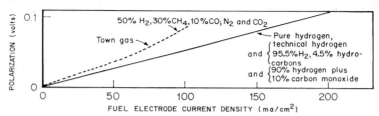

Figure 5-17. The effect of various fuel gases on the polarization at the fuel electrode (200°C; $5N$ KOH; 620 psi).

fuel gases on polarization at the fuel electrode; the curve for technical hydrogen, and also for the mixture of 90 per cent hydrogen and 10 per cent carbon monoxide, is identical with that for pure hydrogen, over short periods of time. "Technical hydrogen" is gas which is produced as a by-product in oil refineries, from the "platforming process."

Present Design

In 1957, the National Research Development Corporation of Great Britain agreed to finance the development and construction of a unit developing 5 to 10 kw, complete with automatic controls, and a contract was placed with Marshall of Cambridge, England.

It was decided to construct a 10-in. diameter cell and it has been in operation since March 1958. The present electrode design has already been described. Axial ports were drilled in the rim to admit the two gases and the electrolyte, as shown in Figure 5-18. When the electrodes are bolted together in the correct order, with rings to provide space for the electrolyte and flat discs of metal to separate the hydrogen from the oxygen in the adjacent cell, they form a battery, the voltage of which depends upon the number of cells connected in series. Radial ports for admitting gas or elec-

Figure 5-18. Electrolyte side of 10-in. diameter electrode.

trolyte from the axial ports to each cell are provided simply by slotting the gaskets. A distributor plate is provided either at one end or in the center of the cell-pack to conduct the gases and electrolyte into and out of the battery. The whole assembly is bolted up between two ribbed-end plates, with electrical insulation between the ends of the pack and the end plates. Electrical connections are silver-soldered onto each electrode, and the inter-cell connections are made externally; the main connections are of course made to the electrodes at each end of the pack.

Up to 40 cells have been operated in series (see Figure 5-19), and no special difficulties have been encountered with, for example, sealing of the joints, excessive shunt currents between cells, excessive electrolysis in the electrolyte ports, etc. But more experience will have to be obtained with large multi-cell packs before reliable results can be quoted.

Development of Control Gear

Control of gas admission has always been a problem, as a very delicate pressure balance has to be maintained between the two gases in the battery. A system has now been worked out whereby the pressure of the oxygen remains constant under all conditions of load; this is achieved by means of a standard two-stage reducing valve. The hydrogen has to be admitted at precisely the correct rate, so that the two gas pressures are balanced to within a few inches of the water gauge. This is accomplished by means of an accurate differential pressure meter, which actuates a power-operated valve to admit the hydrogen; the valve-opening is controlled by a servo mechanism operated by compressed air. Some experience has been obtained with this gear which works extremely well. Figure 5-20 shows various items

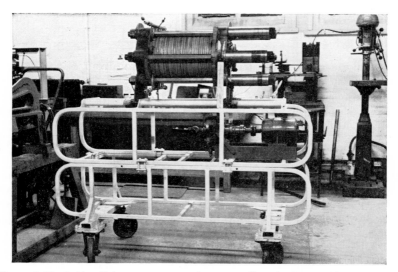

Figure 5-19. A 40-cell battery mounted on a trolley; hydrogen blower mounted underneath.

Figure 5-20. Control gear mounted on front of protective framework.

which make up this control gear mounted on the front of the protective framework enclosing the cell pack.

Much thought has also been given to the problem of removing water, at the same rate at which it is formed. Previously this has been achieved by circulating the hydrogen steam mixture by thermosyphonic action, the steam being condensed out in a small vessel outside the lagging. To do this in a large battery however would require large hydrogen circulating pipes and ports. Thus it was decided to use a small hydrogen blower. A glandless form of drive was considered necessary, in view of the difficulty of preventing hydrogen leakage with a standard type of gland. A magnetically driven pump with a sealing shroud of thin nonmagnetic metal has been employed successfully for some time; it can be seen mounted underneath the battery shown in Figure 5-19. The rate at which the condensate is removed from the system is controlled by switching the blower on and off at intervals, the switch being controlled by a second differential pressure meter which operates on the pressure difference between the hydrogen in the system and the electrolyte. In this way, removal of water is controlled by the total volume of electrolyte which should of course be kept approximately constant. The condensate collects in a small vessel, from which it is released periodically by a level-sensing device such as a capacitance probe. The main parts of this gear, which can be also seen in Figure 5-20, have been in operation and appear to work perfectly well. Until more experience is obtained with this gear, the main level gauges will be retained, but eventually it should be possible to remove them.

The initial heating of the battery is accomplished by electric heaters mounted on the end plates and around the main body of the battery inside the lagging. Various ways have been suggested for maintaining the battery at a constant temperature when on load, but the simplest undoubtedly is to allow cold air to circulate around the battery, inside the lagging, the amount of cold air introduced depending on the temperature of the cell pack.

Lastly, there is the problem of removing gas from the electrolyte system. It is difficult to prevent some generation of hydrogen and oxygen by electrolysis in the common electrolyte ports, although insulation with PTFE helps considerably in this respect. Moreover, there is always the possibility that an electrode may leak, thus allowing gas to enter into the electrolyte system. This is prevented by a level-sensing device, which releases any gas that may collect at the top of the electrolyte system, by means of a solenoid operated valve.

These controls may seem somewhat complicated and expensive, but there is no doubt that they can be made to work. They should not be any more complex with a larger battery and would then represent only a small proportion of the cost of the entire plant.

Advantages and Applications

In view of what has been said, it is unlikely that this type of battery could be competitive with existing types of accumulators in small sizes, owing to the high cost of the control gear in comparison with the over-all cost of the plant. Also, it would be difficult, in very small sizes, to keep the cells up to the working temperature unless they were on load continuously and unless very efficient heat insulation were employed. It is difficult to quote exact figures for minimum sizes until more experience is obtained, but a power output as small as 100 watts is believed to be feasible with really good lagging.

Another factor which should be considered is that it cannot compete with lead accumulators on a weight basis unless the length of time of discharge is greater than about 1 hr; however, for longer periods, the saving in weight becomes increasingly important, as shown in Figure 5-21. The figures for conventional accumulators are somewhat out-of-date, but the general picture today is undoubtedly about the same. It is on a weight basis that the hydrogen-oxygen battery should show an advantage over conventional accumulators. A curve for a Diesel engine with fuel is also included, and this shows that it is difficult to compete on a weight basis with a power generator that gets oxygen from the atmosphere. However, it is important to keep in mind that both accumulators and internal combustion engines have a great many years of careful development behind them, whereas the fuel cell is still in its infancy.

The fuel cell weight of 50 lb/kw shown in Figure 5-21 was worked out for a large battery developing about 44 kw; this weight to power ratio will not be achieved in the small experimental unit now being built, and it would be unwise to hazard a guess about this until it is completed. In the design of the unit, the first requirement has been that it should work—rather than that it should have minimum weight or volume.

As regards power per unit volume, the figure of 8.2 kw/ft³ of internal cell volume has been quoted for a cell voltage of 0.68, and 10 kw/ft³ for a cell voltage of 0.62; a figure of 3 kw/ft³ for the whole battery, without control gear, was quoted by an independent body some years ago, for a cell voltage of 0.8.

It has always been hoped that some specialized application will arise—one for which a fuel cell is particularly suited. In this connection, the pos-

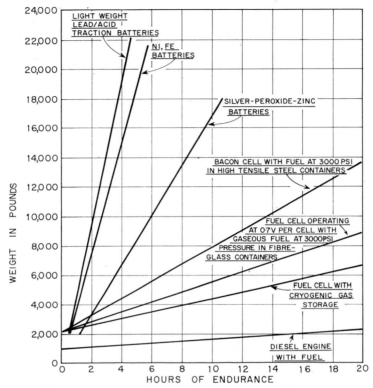

Figure 5-21. Relationship between weight and endurance for 44 kw. cell.

sible use of fuel cells in satellites and space vehicles is of great interest. Then, when further experience has been obtained, it should be possible to enter the commercial field in competition with storage batteries.

It would seem that fuel cells of this type are most suitable for traction purposes, both road and rail. The combination of a battery and direct current series-wound motor provides an ideal propulsion unit for many types of vehicle, the limiting factor thus far being the weight of the battery. The gases would probably be generated by electrolysis of water, and in this connection the development of an efficient high pressure electrolyzer in Germany is of interest. It is well known that the cost of electrical power from the National grid is considerably less than that of power produced in a gasoline engine, and this is of special importance where the vehicle is subject to repeated starts and stops.

Further, if power is generated on a large scale from nuclear energy, the cost of the electricity will be primarily due to the capital cost of the plant rather than to that of the nuclear fuel and the need for some type of large-scale storage will become increasingly important, as little will be gained by shutting down the plants during times of light load.

This type of fuel cell also has other advantages: (1) it is able to take large overloads at reduced efficiency without damage; (2) it is silent and free from vibration in operation; (3) it has very few moving parts and the "exhaust" is only water; (4), the "charging" process merely consists of refilling with the two gases, a very rapid process.

With the advent of new methods of storing hydrogen and oxygen, either in liquid form, or in the former case, as a compressed gas at a very low temperature, it would seem conceivable that vehicles could be propelled over long distance with fuel cells. In view of the rapid depletion of the world's oil supplies, the development of a practical fuel cell should, in the author's opinion, be given high priority.

Acknowledgment

The author would like to thank his colleagues who have given invaluable help in the preparation of this chapter and in particular Dr. R. G. H. Watson, now at the Admiralty Materials Laboratory, Holton Heath, England.

He would also like to thank the Electrical Research Association and the Ministry of Power for valuable financial assistance over many years of research; also Messrs. Marshall of Cambridge, who are now providing facilities for the development work and who have given all possible advice and help; and specially the National Research Development Corporation which is now financing the development work, and has kindly given permission for the publication of this material.

References

1. Grove, W. R., *Phil. Mag.*, No. 3, **14**, 139 (1839).
2. Mond, L., and Langer, C., *Proc. Roy. Soc. London*, **46**, 296–308 (1989).
3. Davtyan, O. K., Direct Conversion of Chemical Energy of Fuel into Electrical Energy (in Russian), Academy of Sciences, Moscow. 1947; E. R. A. Translation Ref. Trans./IB. 884 (1949).
4. Kordesch, K., and Marko, A., *Oesterr. Chem. Ztg.*, **52**, 125–131 (1951).
5. Bacon, F. T., *Beama J.*, **6**, 61 (1954); Bacon, F. T., and Forrest, J. S., Trans. Fifth World Power Conference (Vienna). Div. 3, Section K, paper 119K/4; Watson, R. G. H., *Research*, **7**, 34 (1954).
6. Verwey, E. J. W., "Semi-Conducting Materials," pp. 151–161, Butterworths Scientific Publications Ltd., 1951.
7. Fry, T. M., private communication.
8. Bowen, E. C., *J. Inst. Elec. Engrs.*, **90**, 473 (1943).

6. High-Temperature Fuel Cells

G. H. J. Broers and J. A. A. Ketelaar

Central Technical Institute T.N.O.
The Hague, Netherlands

Investigation of Davtyan-type Cells

Experimental work on high temperature fuel cells was undertaken at the University of Amsterdam in 1951 with a thorough investigation of electrolyte mixtures proposed by the Russian scientist Davtyan.[1] Most probably, Davtyan's attack on the problem of electrolyte preparation was inspired by earlier work of Baur and Preis,[2] who tried to prepare solid electrolytes on the basis of the so-called "Nernst mass" (85 per cent ZrO_2, 15 per cent Y_2O_3) and similar mixtures, containing the oxides of cerium, lanthanum and tungsten. These electrolytes, however, did not possess a sufficient electrolytic conductivity at reasonable temperatures ($< 1000°C$) and did not prove to be invariant against the reducing action of coke or fuel gases such as hydrogen and carbon monoxide.

The principal mixtures employed by Davtyan all contained monazite sand (mineral sand, mainly constituted from the ortho-phosphates of cerium, lanthanum and thorium), which was baked with sodium carbonate and later with tungsten trioxide and soda glass, in order to increase the conductivity and the mechanical strength. The electrolyte, finally chosen by Davtyan, was composed of a baked mixture of 43 per cent calcinated Na_2CO_3, 27 per cent monazite, 20 per cent WO_3 and 10 per cent soda glass. Investigations, based upon chemical analysis, conductivity measurements and differential thermal analysis resulted in the following conclusions.

(1) Na_2CO_3 and monazite sand, on baking, react according to Equation (1):

$$3Na_2CO_3 + 2\ MPO_4 \xrightarrow{\ (850°C)\ } 2Na_3PO_4 + M_2O_3 + 3CO_2 \qquad (1)$$

(M stands for a trivalent rare earth metal).

(2) The "stoichiometrical" weight ratio according to Equation (1) is about 17 Na_2CO_3 to 27 monazite when the effect of impurities in the mineral and the Ce-La-Th ratio is taken into account.

78

(3) The excess Na_2CO_3 in Davtyan's mixture reacts with WO_3 according to Equation (2):

$$Na_2CO_3 + WO_3 \rightarrow Na_2WO_4 + CO_2 \qquad (2)$$

For 20 weight parts WO_3, 9 parts of Na_2CO_3 are required.

(4) Consequently, from the total of 43 parts Na_2CO_3 $(43 - 17 - 9 = 17)$ 17 parts are in excess with regard to monazite and WO_3. Since the quantity of soda glass, namely, 10 parts, will never convert more than about 9 parts of Na_2CO_3 into Na_2SiO_3, at least 8 parts of Na_2CO_3 still remain unaltered in the baked electrolyte. This could be verified by chemical analysis.

The reaction product, after baking Davtyan's mixture, will therefore consist of the following components: Na_3PO_4, Na_2CO_3, Na_2WO_4, Na_2SiO_3 and oxides CeO_2, La_2O_3 and ThO_2, apart from impurities of minor importance.

It was found that the simple eutectic melting point of the system Na_2CO_3–Na_3PO_4 was at 780°C and 90 mole per cent Na_2CO_3. The binary system Na_2WO_4–Na_3PO_4, however, showed eutectics at 655 and 640°C, separated by a largely dissociated compound Na_2WO_4–Na_3PO_4 with a melting point of 663°C (Figure 6-1).

Some conductivity *vs.* temperature curves of fired carbonate (c), monazite (m), WO_3 (w) and glass (g) mixtures are shown in Figure 6-2. They all show breaks in the temperature range 500 to 650°C due to the over-

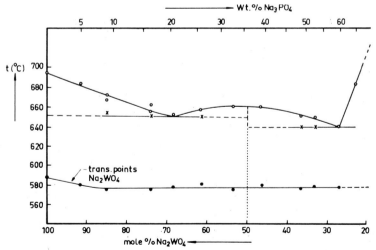

Figure 6-1. Melting point diagram of the system Na_2W_4-Na_3PO_4.

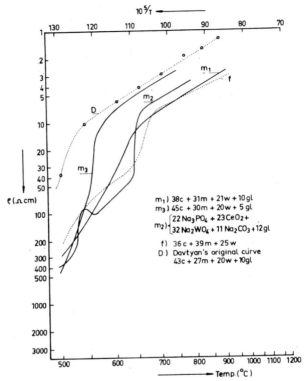

Figure 6-2. Conductivity curves of Na_2CO_3-monazite-WO_3-glass systems.

whelming effect of the formation of liquid eutectic phases upon the conductivity.

The conclusion can be drawn, that Davtyan's "solid electrolytes" are not real solids at their operating temperature, but that they consist of a solid porous frame of high melting rare earth oxides, in which eutectic salt mixtures of molten carbonates, phosphates, tungstates and silicates are impregnated to form the electrolytically conducting phase.

Investigations of fuel cells according to Davtyan's description[1] showed that they had a number of serious disadvantages when run on town gas and air at 650 to 800°C for a few days.

(1) All WO_3-containing electrolytes showed pronounced reduction phenomena on the fuel gas side, resulting in formation of lower tungsten oxides (grey-greenish color) with additional open pores and small cracks in the electrolyte disk. Open circuit voltages fell from 1.0 to 1.1 volts initially to

less than 0.8 volt in a few hours and to less than 0.5 volt in a few days. Current densities could not be increased to more than 5 ma/sq cm. It was found also that Na_2WO_4 was partly converted into Na_2CO_3 .

(2) Sintered Fe_2O_3–Fe_3O_4-clay mixtures, proposed as air cathodes by Davtyan, were found to be oxidized within 24 hr to Fe_2O_3-clay systems with very low electronic conductivity.

(3) Sintered Fe–Fe_3O_4-clay mixtures, proposed as fuel gas anodes, were found to be reduced to Fe-clay mixtures after they were in use for 24 hr.

(4) Volume changes, associated with the direct attack of gases on the electrolyte and the electrodes, caused inhomogeneities and cracks in all essential parts of the cells, so that they were destroyed after being in operation for periods of 24 to 72 hr, apart from the earlier mentioned reduction phenomena.

It is quite obvious that one of the principal demands for long-term operation of high temperature cells, i.e., invariance of both electrolyte and electrodes, never can be fulfilled with the Davtyan-type cell.

Further research was therefore directed toward the development of cells with electrolytes and electrodes with permanent stability against the action of the reacting gases and their combustion products.

Possibilities with Regard to High Temperature Cell Electrolytes

Since formation and electrolytic transport of positive gas ions such as H^+ or CO^+ are highly improbable for energetic reasons, the net electrolytic mass transport must proceed by $O^=$ ions, traveling from cathode to anode. The most straightforward way would be the application of a solid $O^=$ ionic conductor of the Nernst-mass type, which owes its conductivity to imperfections in the crystal lattice. The solid state of the electrolyte would prevent danger of electrode "drowning," which is always present with liquid electrolytes. Moreover, no electrolytic concentration polarization would occur if both the conductivity and the oxygen pressure were sufficiently high.

However, the contradictory demands placed upon such solids are evident both from theoretical considerations and from Baur's experiments. Solid conductors should have a large unipolar ionic conductivity at relatively low temperatures, the electronic conductivity must be negligible, and they should be inert against the prolonged action of the reactants and their products. Moreover, they should have good mechanical strength, good ceramic properties and must be completely gas tight.

Baur's work has shown that the combination good anionic unipolar conductivity below 1000°C and inertness against fuel gases cannot be realized. The latter requires a strong metal-oxygen bond, of ionic character, such as is present in oxides of alkaline earth metals or the rare earth metals. The strong bonding prevents the mobility of the relatively large $O^=$ ions (radius 1.45Å) from being great, even if lattice defects are created by mixed crystal formation. The very high melting points ($>1500°C$) of the oxides considered indicate that there is little hope of obtaining sufficient $O^=$ conductivity (say of the order 5 to 1 ohm cm) at temperatures below $1000°C$.

Considering fused salts as electrolytes, it should be kept in mind that the reaction products of energy delivering high temperature cells will be mainly CO_2 and steam when carbonaceous gases are the fuels.

This excludes the use of salts having volatile dissociation products at the operating temperature. For example, an electrolyte of sodium-potassium chloride may be considered. The continuous steam formation at the anode of the working cell will finally convert the MCl (M = alkali metal) into MOH, by the following reaction

$$MCl + H_2O \leftrightarrows MOH + HCl \tag{3}$$

although generally equilibrium takes place on the left side of the equation. In addition, CO_2 converts the MOH into M_2CO_3.

Direct experimental evidence obtained shows that fused chloride and fused sulfate electrolytes are indeed converted into carbonates after the cell has been in operation for a few days, while HCl or SO_2–SO_3 mixtures escaped from the anode compartments of the cells under investigation. Salts such as phosphates, chlorides, sulfates and nitrates therefore cannot be considered as stable electrolytes, unless their dissociation products (P_2O_5, HCl, SO_3, NO_2) are supplied at the cathodic side of the cell.

Salts such as silicates or borates will not be decomposed; however, they show severe concentration polarization under current drain. This can be explained by assuming the cathodic reaction to be, e.g.,

$$2e^- + \tfrac{1}{2}O_2 + 2M^+ \rightarrow M_2O \tag{4a}$$

while the anodic reaction is

$$SiO_3^= + CO \rightarrow SiO_2 + CO_2 + 2e^- \tag{4b}$$

M_2O and SiO_2, which accumulate at the cathode and anode, respectively, will recombine by diffusion in the melt, but generally the diffusion velocity is too small to keep up with a technically acceptable current drain. Polarization is therefore inevitable unless SiO_2 is supplied at the cathode in some other way, which would present a rather difficult problem in a technical battery.

It is clear that fused carbonates are fundamentally the best adapted salts for high-temperature cells since decomposition by action of CO_2 is impossible and concentration polarization can be eliminated by supplying CO_2 (withdrawn from the combustion products) to the cathodic air (oxygen).

Recent quantitative measurements have shown that during the galvanic combustion of H_2 or CO with air $+ CO_2$, 1 mole of CO_2 is taken up at the cathode and liberated at the anode for every mole of H_2 or CO oxidized at the anode:

$$\text{cathode: } 2e^- + \tfrac{1}{2}O_2 + CO_2 \rightarrow CO_3^= \tag{5a}$$

$$\text{anode: } CO_3^= + H_2 \rightarrow H_2O + CO_2 + 2e^- \tag{5b}$$

The transfer of the $O^=$ ions thus proceeds in the form of $CO_3^=$ ions, obtained from gaseous O_2 and CO_2 at the cathode-electrolyte interface.

Although the CO_2 addition to air introduces technical problems, it cannot be considered as a fundamental difficulty because of its abundant presence in the exhaust gases of the cell.

Cell Construction and Stability

In our research, the electrolyte employed was a mixture of lithium-, sodium- and/or potassium carbonate, impregnated in a porous sintered disk of magnesium oxide. No special care was taken with regard to the purity of the MgO, the usual trade product "Magnesia Usta" being used. Sintering took place at 1200°C, after a presintering stage at the same temperature. The disks obtained were not very hard because of the relatively low firing temperature. They had a volume porosity of 40 to 50 per cent. After impregnation, the alkali carbonate content was usually about 40 per cent by weight, which indicates that not all the MgO pores were filled with the liquid. Construction of the cell is shown in Figure 6-3.

The impregnated disk (4) was covered on both sides with thin layers of metal powders (5). The powders were prepared by reduction of the corresponding oxides in a H_2 or CO atmosphere, the reduction temperature being chosen equal to or slightly above the operating temperature of the cell, in order to prevent a further sintering of the powders during the working period of the cell. Since electrode reactions are confined to areas very close to the geometrical "three-phase lines" bordering the metal-, electrolyte- and gas phases, powder layers can be kept as thin as allowed by the demands of good mutual electric contact and the prevention of "drowning." It was found that the powder layers could be made less than about 1 mm thick when additional care was taken. This consisted in covering the powder layers with silver wire gauzes (6) (or, at the anode, with iron, nickel or copper gauze) to maintain contact, and covering the gauzes in turn with

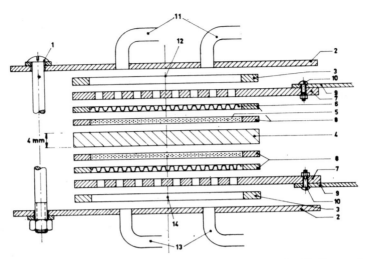

Figure 6-3. High temperature laboratory cell ("exploded view"). See explanation in text.

firm perforated stainless steel disks (7) of 1 mm thickness to prevent deformation. Terminal wires (9) of silver were screwed (10) onto the latter. The assembly was completed by gaskets of mica (8) and asbestos (3) and by steel covers (2) with pipes (11, 13) for circulation of the gases. Screws (1) with appropriate mica-isolating rings connected the cell parts.

Cells of this type could be run continuously for several months, operating between 550 and 700°C on town gas, hydrogen, carbon monoxide and natural gas. The best specimen had a "life" of six months, although the open-circuit voltage had fallen from 1.1 volts initially to 0.90 volt (on town gas/air + CO_2). The cell resistance, as measured with an a.c. bridge, had increased in the same period from 0.3 to 1.5 ohm (10 sq cm geometrical electrode area).

Slow deterioration was caused by a gradual loss of carbonate melt, both by direct vaporization of CO_2, Li_2O, Na_2O and K_2O, and by chemical reactions of the soda with gasket materials. The direct vaporization could be verified by chemical analysis of the carbonate mixture, from which the lithium loss was found to be greater than the potassium or sodium loss. This could be suppressed to a considerable extent by maintaining a small CO_2 pressure in both gas rooms and the outer furnace atmosphere. Reactions between the melt and the gaskets could not be avoided, however.

In the opinion of the authors, the loss of electrolyte is the main, and probably the only cause of slow deterioration of cell performance. In one instance, where the MgO disk of a cell was reimpregnated during its operation (after three months), it showed the same performance as during the first week of its life. Obviously the electrodes were not drowned, neither had they suffered from the prolonged galvanic action.

The increasing loss of fused salts led to increasing gas leakage across the disks, so that the ratio of electrochemical turnover to total turnover decreased and local galvanic action at the places where leakage occurred lowered the cell voltage. Moreover, cell resistance increased, and, in some cases, excessive heat evolution by direct reaction of the gases caused total destruction of the cell. Therefore, conclusions about performances of electrodes and fuel gases were usually made in the first month of operation, the best results also being the most reliable.

Detection of Suitable Electrodes

Experiments with cells having two electrodes of equal constitution, but appreciably different areas (about 5 to 1), were undertaken to detect suitable electrode metals. By passing the fuel gas and oxygen alternately over the small and the large electrode, terminal voltage, V_t vs. current density, i, characteristics could be obtained which gave a direct indication of polarization differences. An example is given in Figure 6-4. Silver electrodes obviously are better for oxygen than for hydrogen or carbon monoxide at temperatures below 700°C.

Platinum electrodes were found to be slightly better for hydrogen than for oxygen, though at 700°C the difference was negligible.

The logical combination of these results led to the testing of a cell with a silver-oxygen-CO_2 and a platinum-hydrogen electrode (Figure 6-5).

Curves 1 and 2 for $H_2/O_2 + CO_2$ galvanic couples reveal the absence of polarization, other than the purely ohmic drop, up to current densities of 150 ma/sq cm at 500°C. This follows from the fact that a correction for the ohmic cell resistance, as determined with alternating current (1000 cps), transforms them in practically horizontal lines (1' and 2'). Similar experiments with air + CO_2 (oxygen pressure 0.17 atm) have shown that under these circumstances the polarization of the silver electrodes at 500°C is also negligible. Thus the silver powder can be considered as an ideal $O_2 + CO_2$ electrode in any carbonate fuel cell operating at 500°C or higher.

Curves 3 and 3' show the necessity of a cathodic CO_2 supply, as discussed earlier. Curves 4 and 4' and 5 and 5' reveal polarization of the platinum electrode with carbon monoxide at 600°C.

Once it had been found that the silver-oxygen electrode does not polarize,

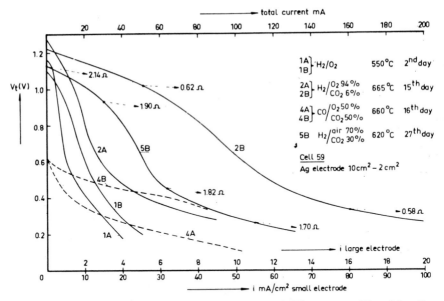

Figure 6-4. i-V_t curves of a cell with Ag electrodes of different area (10 and 2 cm²).
Curve A: fuel gas passed over small electrode, i.e., large anodic current densities.
Curve B: large cathodic c.d. 's.
Silver is a better oxygen electrode than a fuel gas electrode. The slope of the dotted
arrows correspond to the a.c. resistance of the cell.

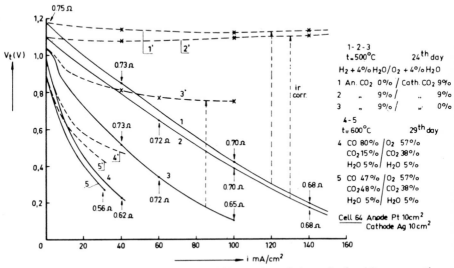

Figure 6-5. i-V_t curves of cell 64 with Pt anode and Ag cathode. After correction
for the ohmic drop, curves 1' and 2' do not show polarization. (See text for further
description.)

comparative experiments with different anodic metal powders could be undertaken with regard to their usefulness as H_2, CO and CH_4 electrodes.

For hydrogen, platinum and nickel appear to be suitable. For carbon monoxide, the following series of metals with decreasing galvanic activity at 700°C was found:

$$Pt > \text{platinized Fe or Ni} > Fe > Ni > Co > Cu > Cr > Mn$$

The series, however, should be regarded with some reserve, since differences in particle size may play an important role and the general reproducibility of results with similarly constructed cells has not been too good. Moreover, above 750°C, the differences in performance become negligible.

For CH_4, no satisfactory electrode metal has been found for temperatures below 750°C. If, however, steam is added to the CH_4, nickel electrodes appear to be suitable. This effect may be ascribed to the nickel-catalyzed formation of hydrogen and carbon monoxide, according to:

$$CH_4 + H_2O \leftrightarrows CO + 3H_2 \qquad (6)$$

It should be stressed that, theoretically, equilibrium reactions such as (6) do not introduce important losses in potential electrical energy since the associated free enthalpy change is small compared to that of the ideal galvanic combustion of CH_4 with oxygen. This can be seen at once by comparing the standard emf's (in reference to O_2) of different fuel gases:

Fuel	H_2	C (to CO_2)	CO	CH_4	C_2H_6
E_0 at 800°K (volts)	1.05	1.03	1.10	1.04	1.07
E_0 at 1000°K (volts)	1.00	1.03	1.01	1.04	1.08

Since, at 1000°K, both $E_0(H_2)$ and $E_0(CO)$ are only slightly less than $E_0(CH_4)$, the losses in ideal electrical energy, associated with reaction (6), will be small. Similar arguments hold for the reaction

$$CO + H_2O \leftrightarrows CO_2 + H_2 \qquad (7)$$

Hydrogen is by far the most galvanically reactive gas and moreover, its diffusion constant is five to eight times greater than that of CO or CH_4. Therefore, it may be expected that in CH_4–CO–H_2 mixtures the principal electrochemical reaction will be the oxidation of H_2 to steam. Consequently, the equilibria (6) or (7) will shift to the right-hand side whereby fresh hydrogen is formed. The essential kinetic problem is therefore to see that the shift rate of (6) and (7) keeps up with the galvanic conversion rate of the hydrogen, or, in other words, with the current density possible with hydrogen gas. Since reactions (6) and (7) are not confined to the three-phase (electrochemical) sites but may proceed over the full electrode surface, there is no fundamental reason why methane cannot be burnt with sufficient velocity. The electrode in this case should be both a good methane-steam "reforming" catalyst and a good hydrogen electrode. As experiments have demonstrated, nickel powder serves fairly good for this double function.

A further study of the important function of catalytic CO-steam and CH_4-steam reactions is a major point in our present research.

Significance of Current Density-Terminal Voltage Characteristics

Characteristics are most commonly used as a measure of cell performance. Attention should be given to the fact that only stationary values have real significance. For instance, adsorbed quantities of hydrogen from earlier experiments may obscure the real behavior of CH_4 if the observation time is too short. It is generally better to start a measurement with a large current density and decrease it afterward, than to do the reverse. Measurement in both directions is the safest way. Another important point is that in high temperature cells the partial pressures of the reaction products increase with increasing conversion of the fuel gases. The terminal voltage therefore is a function of both the gas feed rate and the current density, whenever the gas supply is continuous.

In experiments described in the literature, one gets the impression that the gas feed rates are nearly always substantially larger than their consumption rates (which are proportional to the current drawn). This way of carrying out experiments is necessary whenever there is some leakage across the electrolyte, in order to "flush the electrodes," but it means that the reaction products cannot accumulate. A characteristic, thus obtained, does not give more than a snapshot of optimal operating conditions if fuel gases, practically free of reaction products, are fed into the cell. "Voltage efficiencies" (actual voltage/theoretical voltage), derived in this way, overestimate the real performance since the fuel gas must be at least 80 per cent converted for any practical application of a cell battery.

This is illustrated in Figure 6-6, which shows the general course of the theoretical cell voltage E and the actual voltages V_t as functions of the conversion degree λ of the fuel gas and the current density i (similar arguments hold for the cathodic gas). As a result of increasing polarization at increasing λ and i, the V_t curves fall more rapidly than does the E curve, and complete conversion at non-zero i therefore cannot be reached.

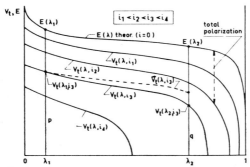

Figure 6-6. Terminal voltage V_t as a function of current density i and conversion degree of the fuel gas. As a consequence of polarization, not all the gas can be converted. The true voltage efficiency (between λ_1 and λ_2) is the ratio of the areas under the V_t curve and the E curve, bordered by the λ axis, p and q. The ratio $V_t(\lambda_1)/E(\lambda_1)$ overestimates the cell performance.

Dotted curve: "average terminal voltage" V (at $i = i_3$).

A "voltage efficiency," as just described, corresponds with the ratio V_t/E at $\lambda = \lambda_1$, while a more realistic measurement would be the ratio $\int V_t \, d\lambda / \int E \, d\lambda$, for instance, over the range λ_1 to λ_2.

A suitable method for obtaining results of this kind is the measurement of a number of characteristics, corresponding with gases of different λ's, at relatively rapid feed rates.

In that case the results correspond to the behavior of a series-connected battery, in which only a small fraction of fuel gas has been oxidized in each cell.

Another method would be adjustment of the fuel gas feed rates to values slightly higher than the rates which correspond with the current drawn. Then the terminal voltage will be a realistic measure with regard to virtually complete galvanic turnover in one pass. However, the observed voltage in this case is a mixed potential difference, since local action between spots of different gas concentrations inevitably will occur. Moreover, experimentally this method fails altogether in case there is some direct leakage across the electrolyte. (A total current of 1 amp from a small laboratory cell requires a minimal feed rate of 445 ml/hr of H_2 or CO at 20°C and 1 atm; if the leakage amounts to a few ml per hour only, severe local action may be the result when the actual feed rate is 450 ml/hr.)

The experiments were therefore carried out with gas feed rates considerably greater than the electrochemical rate of turnover.

Some Experimental Results

Hydrogen containing up to 50 mole per cent H_2O can deliver current densities of 50 ma/sq cm at 0.80 to 0.70 volt, and 100 ma/sq cm at 0.60 to 0.40 volt on nickel powder electrodes at 600 to 650°C, with air + CO_2 as a cathodic gas passed over silver powder electrodes.

The nickel-hydrogen electrode appears to be rather insensitive to direct leakage across the electrolyte, most probably because of its large adsorption capacity. Cells could be run for several months at 650°C under steady conditions, the only obvious deterioration being a slow loss in electrolyte which results in a corresponding decrease in terminal voltage and increase in internal resistance. Polarization, other than purely ohmic decreases, appeared to be negligible. The effect of cathodic CO_2 is illustrated in Figure 6-7 and requires no comment.

Methane is much more difficult to handle. So far, nickel electrodes at temperatures of 750°C or higher have been found promising if steam is added to the CH_4 (see p. 85).

At 770°C, a CH_4–H_2O mixture with 30 mole per cent H_2O gave the following results:

current density, ma/sq cm	0	20	40	60
terminal voltage, v	0.98	0.80	0.63	0.50

Recent experiments with cells of a different design have demonstrated also that methane-steam mixtures at 650 to 700°C can give quite good results on active nickel electrodes. This study is being continued.

Experiments with CO–CO_2 mixtures have revealed that at 650 to 700°C iron or iron-nickel electrodes are very sensitive to a small leakage of oxygen from the cathodic side, especially when the CO_2 content of the CO is over 50 mole per cent. The open-circuit voltage is greatly decreased below the reversible value. Reversely, the silver-oxygen-CO_2 electrode is far less sensitive to CO leakage, probably because of its observed excellent cathodic activity.

It was found that the performance of CO–CO_2 mixtures improved considerably if the oxygen content of the cathodic gas was reduced to a few volume per cent. By means of this artifice, the characteristics of Figure 6-8 could be obtained (starting with the lowest CO content). According to the figure, CO—CO_2 mixtures can be burnt at 720°C to a final CO content of 5 mole per cent at 10 ma/sq cm, and to a content of 10 mole per cent at 21 ma/sq cm.

Assuming that a mixture of x_i moles CO and $1 - x_i$ moles CO_2 enters a

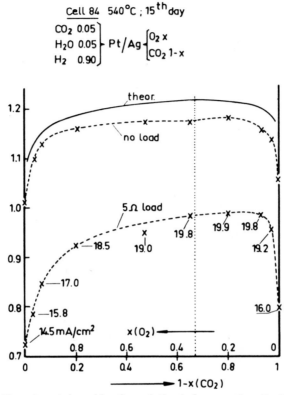

Figure 6-7. Experimental verification of the influence of cathodic CO_2 on the terminal voltage of a H_2-O_2 cell. Solid curve: theoretical values of the emf. Broken curves: observed values of V_0 and V_t.

series-connected cell battery, and that x_f moles of CO escape in the outlet gases, the quantity of CO_2 in the latter gases can be written as $(1 - x_i) + (1 + \varphi)(x_i - x_f)$, when φ denotes the number of moles of *cathodic* CO_2 needed per mole anodic CO to prevent excessive concentration polarization under the prevailing conditions. In the strictly reversible cell, $\varphi = 0$; in the most unfavorable case, $\varphi = 1$; in practice it will have a value $0 < \varphi < 1$, depending on the diffusivity of CO_2 across the electrolyte, for which no exact data are known. Assuming $\varphi = 1$, the CO fraction in the outlet gases is

$$\gamma_{CO} = x_f/(1 + x_i - x_f).$$

If $\varphi = 0$, $\gamma_{CO} = x_f$.

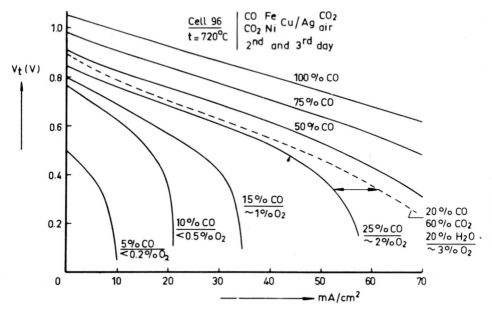

Figure 6-8. i-V_t characteristics of cell 96 at 720°C. Curves measured at optimal conditions: oxygen content of cathodic gas adapted to the CO content of the anodic gas, in order to avoid leakage effects.

TABLE 6-1

Voltage and thermal efficiencies of galvanic CO combustion at 720°C according to Figure 6-8. Fuel gas: $CO + CO_2$ mixture. $x_i = 0.75$ mole CO; $1 - x_i = 0.25$ mole CO_2 , x_f is the number of moles CO that cannot be converted.

i ma/sq cm	10		20		30		40	
	$\varphi = 0$	$\varphi = 1$	$\varphi = 0$	$\varphi = 1$	$\varphi = 0$	$\varphi = 1$	$\varphi = 0$	$\varphi = 1$
x_f	0.05	0.08	0.10	0.16	0.15	0.23	0.20	0.24
$\overline{V}_t$, volts	0.79		0.72		0.65		0.60	
$\eta_{volt.}$ CO	0.78		0.71		0.64		0.59	
$\eta_{thermal}$ CO	0.54		0.49		0.44		0.41	
α	0.36	0.61	0.34	0.59	0.32	0.56	0.30	0.52
$\eta_{thermal}$ carbon (integr. system)	0.75	0.71	0.66	0.60	0.65	0.55	0.52	0.44

The average voltage, associated with the galvanic combustion of CO can be written as

$$\bar{V}_t = \left[\int_{x_f}^{x_i} V_t \, dx \right] / (x_i - x_f)$$

(compare Figure 6-6).

This voltage can be found by graphic integration, when the curves of Figure 6-8 are being transformed in a set of V_t vs. $(x_i - x_f)$ curves (with the current density as parameter) similar to Figure 6-6.

The voltage efficiency of the CO combustion may now be defined as $\eta_{\text{voltage}} = \bar{V}_t/E_0$, E_0 being the standard emf of CO-oxygen couple at the operating temperature, namely, 1.01 volts at 720°C. In the present case, no attention is given to the CO escaping in the outlet gases, but it should be kept in mind that recycling of a part of the outlet gas over coal or coke in an integrated fuel cell-gasification system is the real advantage of such a process.*

Table 6-1 shows the results as derived from Figure 6-8; it is assumed that $x_i = 0.75$, corresponding with the concentration of CO in heterogeneous equilibrium with carbon and CO_2 at 720°C and atmospheric pressure.

The data in the two lowest columns refer to a recycling process of a fraction $(1 - \alpha)$ of the anodic outlet gas over carbon, in order to recover the original CO—CO_2 mixture as anodic fuel gas. The thermal efficiency in this case is based on the heat value of the carbon, the heat value of the CO in the "waste fraction" α being considered as a total loss.

It is clear that a "promising characteristic" as e.g., the 100 per cent CO in Figure 6-8 —0.8 volt at 50 ma/sq cm— tells very little about the practical behavior of CO.

On the other hand, the data obtained may be subject to considerable improvement since they were measured with an imperfect gas-tight cell and rather low oxygen concentrations. Recent experiments with cells of better gas-tightness have demonstrated that open-circuit voltages of over 0.75 volt can be found on gases with only 5 per cent CO, the cathodic gas being air with a CO_2 content of 28 mole per cent. Improvement of electrodes and addition of steam are likely to result in much better current density performances.

References

1. Davtyan, O. K., *Bull. acad. sci. U. R. S. S. Classe sci. tech.* **107,** 215 (1946).
2. Baur, E., and Preis, H., *Z. Elektrochem.*, **43,** 727 (1937); **44,** 695 1938).

---

* Thesis of the author, Chapter 3.

7. Carbonaceous Fuel Cells

H. H. Chambers and A. D. S. Tantram

Sondes Place Research Institute
Dorking, Surrey, England

Introduction

Our studies on fuel cells were started in 1953 under the joint sponsorship of the Ministry of Power and the Central Electricity Authority (now the Central Electricity Generating Board). Additional support has been provided in the last two years by Shell Research Ltd. The object of the work was to develop general-purpose fuel cells to operate on conventional gaseous fuels such as producer gas, town gas, natural gas and vaporized liquid hydrocarbons.

The early work was based on the Davtyan cell, which seemed to possess many of the desirable features of an ideal fuel cell and was claimed to give a good performance.[1] Being a high-temperature cell, it was unlikely to suffer from activation polarization due to low fuel reactivity and its simple and robust design of flat porous diffusion electrodes separated by a solid electrolyte made it very suitable for constructing compact batteries.

Davtyan's claims were not substantiated, mainly because it proved impossible to build cells with low internal resistance. The early experiments also revealed three serious shortcomings: the iron-iron oxide electrodes were unstable and were rapidly oxidized to ferric oxide on the air side and reduced to iron on the fuel side; the electrolyte (a sintered mixture of monazite sand, sodium carbonate, soda glass, tungsten oxide and clay) was not a true solid ionic conductor, but owed its conductivity to the presence of low-melting eutectics in a porous solid matrix; and the electrolyte suffered irreversible chemical changes during long runs. The cell was evidently unnecessarily complex from the chemical standpoint.

Although this early work was abortive, it served to direct attention to the problems which had to be solved before a satisfactory design could be evolved.

Electrolytes and Electrodes

The two functions of the electrolyte are (1) to transport oxygen in ionic form from the air electrode to the fuel electrode, and (2) to provide a gas-impermeable barrier between the two electrodes. An ideal electrolyte would

94

be a solid ionic oxide with anion conductance. Unfortunately all the oxides with well-marked ionic structures have very high melting points and it is only at temperatures near their melting points that they show any marked ionic conductance. For steric reasons, it is usually the cation which is the mobile ion.

The next best thing to a pure oxide electrolyte is a salt which transports oxygen-containing ions. In practice the most satisfactory salts are the alkali metal carbonates in the fused state. With these electrolytes, it is necessary to feed carbon dioxide into the air stream, as suggested by Greger,[2] since otherwise the carbonate is rapidly converted to oxide and the internal resistance of the cell rises.

If possible, the electrodes should be constructed of materials which are chemically inert toward the fuel and air, so that they act as pure gas electrodes. Side reactions of the electrode material are undesirable partly because of the resulting free energy loss and partly because physical changes accompanying such reactions tend to disrupt the electrodes.

The active part of a porous diffusion electrode in contact with a liquid electrolyte is the region of three-phase contact-solid-liquid-gas. The electrode is inactivated if the solid surface is completely covered with electrolyte and it is common practice with low-temperature cells containing aqueous electrolyte to apply a waterproofing treatment to the electrodes. Two methods have been used successfully for preventing electrode flooding in high-temperature cells. In the first, the fused electrolyte is held in the pores of a porous ceramic diaphragm and the electrodes are pressed into contact or otherwise attached to the surface of the diaphragm. If the pore size of the ceramic diaphragm is smaller than that of the electrodes, the electrolyte is prevented from penetrating into the electrodes by surface tension forces. The individual particles forming the porous electrode must be completely nonporous, otherwise they may become "water-logged" even if the large pores remain free.

The second method is the one devised by Bacon[3] for constructing the electrode in two layers; a coarse-pore layer on the gas side and a fine-pore layer in contact with the electrolyte. With this construction free molten electrolyte is used without a diaphragm. The relative pore sizes of the two layers are chosen so that a small excess gas pressure forces the electrolyte to the interface between the two layers and yet the gas does not bubble out through the fine-pore face until a much higher gas pressure is attained.

The Fuel Cell as a Concentration Cell

The theoretical emf of a perfect fuel cell with an oxide electrolyte running on carbon monoxide is given by

$$E = E_0 - \frac{RT}{2F} \ln \frac{P_{CO_2}^2}{P_{CO}^2 P_{O_2}} \tag{1}$$

where P_{CO}, P_{O_2} and P_{CO_2} are the partial pressures of the fuel, oxygen, and reaction product, respectively.

Following Allmand and Ellingham,[4] we can regard the cell as an oxygen concentration cell with a fuel-depolarized anode. The emf is then given by

$$E = E_0 - \frac{RT}{4F} \ln \frac{P'_{O_2}}{P_{O_2}} \tag{2}$$

where P_{O_2} is the oxygen partial pressure at the air electrode and P'_{O_2} the partial pressure of oxygen in equilibrium with the fuel.

This argument can be extended to a carbonate electrolyte cell with a mixed air-CO_2 feed to the air electrode. The cathode reaction is

$$O_2 + 2CO_2 + 4e = 2CO_3^= \tag{3}$$

The anode reaction is

$$2CO_3^= = O_2 + 2CO_2 + 4e \tag{4}$$

followed by reaction of oxygen with the fuel gas.

The net cell reaction is then

$$O_2(P_{O_2}) + 2CO_2(P_{CO_2}) = O_2(P'_{O_2}) + 2CO_2(P'_{CO_2}) \tag{5}$$

where P_{O_2} and P_{CO_2} are the partial pressures at the air electrode and P'_{O_2} and P'_{CO_2} the partial pressures at the fuel electrode. If then the removal of discharged oxygen by the fuel is an equilibrium process, the cell emf is expressed by

$$E = E_0 - \frac{RT}{4F} \ln \frac{P'_{O_2}}{P_{O_2}} - \frac{RT}{2F} \ln \frac{P'_{CO_2}}{P_{CO_2}} \tag{6}$$

The cell is effectively a combined oxygen and carbon dioxide concentration cell in which the primary anodic and cathodic processes are identical. The implication is that the same material should serve for both electrodes, provided it is a good oxidation catalyst. Alternatively, the anode material should be an admixture of cathode material and an oxidation catalyst.

Another corollary of the concentration cell hypothesis is that if the anode material is a good oxidation catalyst, the chemical nature of the fuel is of only secondary importance in determining cell performance. This is borne out by experimental observation that with a given electrode system the cell performance is roughly parallel with the ease of oxidation of the fuel.

For example, with the cells described later the performances are almost identical for hydrogen, carbon monoxide and methanol; kerosene vapor gives a slightly inferior performance; and methane substantially inferior, with evidence of activation polarization.

Quantitative measurements on fuel cells operated as direct concentration cells without fuel show good correspondence between observed emf's and values calculated from Equation (6). The simple cell in Figure 7-1 was made by allowing molten alkali carbonate in a silver crucible to solidify around the open end of a sintered alumina tube with a side arm and a silver wire touching the surface of the electrolyte. The cell was held at a constant temperature with the crucible exposed to the atmosphere and the emf was measured with different air pressures inside the tube. The results at two different temperatures are plotted in Figure 7-2 and are seen to lie very close to the theoretical lines calculated from Equation (6).

In another experiment a disc cell of the type described later was fed with a cathodic gas supply at 1 atm pressure of an air-carbon dioxide mixture with $P_{O_2} = 0.086$ atm and $P_{CO_2} = 0.57$ atm, and with an anodic gas of pure oxygen-free carbon dioxide. A small current was drawn from the cell and adjusted in relation to the gas flow to give an exit gas composition

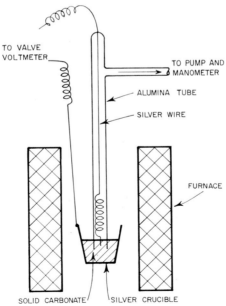

Figure 7-1. Direct concentration cell.

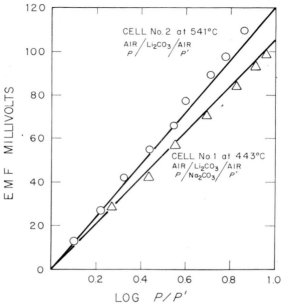

Figure 7-2. Experimental and theoretical open-circuit voltages for direct concentration cells.

from the anode of 0.5 per cent O_2 and 99.9 per cent CO_2. Assuming no polarization, the emf calculated from Equation (6) would have been:

$$+52.7 \text{ mv for the } O_2 \text{ concentration cell}$$
$$-20.7 \text{ mv for the } CO_2 \text{ concentration cell}$$
$$\overline{\quad\quad\quad\quad\quad\quad\quad\quad\quad\quad}$$
$$+32 \quad \text{mv over-all}$$

The measured terminal voltage in the steady state was actually 32 mv.

Finally a cell with a "Pyrex" glass electrolyte, a cathodic gas supply of air at 1 atm pressure and an anodic supply at 1 atm pressure of carbon dioxide containing 0.05 per cent oxygen, gave an emf at 700°C of 118 mv, compared with a theoretical value of 126 mv.

Practical Fuel Cells

These considerations have led to the development of the two types of cell shown diagrammatically in Figures 7-3 and 7-4, both of which are capable of being scaled up in size and built up into compact batteries.

In the porous diaphragm cell (Figure 7-3), the electrolyte is a eutectic mix-

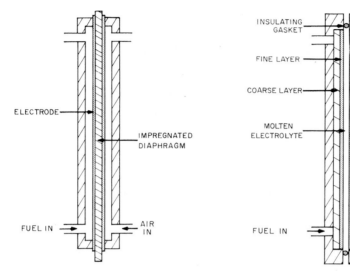

Figure 7-3. Diaphragm cell.   Figure 7-4. Free electrolyte cell.

ture of sodium and lithium carbonates held in a porous sintered magnesia disc. The two electrodes are identical and consist of porous layers of silverized zinc oxide 0.020 in. thick. Other combinations of silver and metal oxides are possible. The electrodes are catalytically active and under the conditions prevailing in the cell they are neither oxidized nor reduced. The porosity of the magnesia disc is 50 per cent and the maximum pore size is 25 microns.

The disc with its attached electrodes is virtually the complete fuel cell. Batteries are built up by sandwiching the discs between recessed metal plates arranged with supply tubes to feed gas and air and carry away reaction products.

In the second type of cell (Figure 7-4), free molten electrolyte is used with two-layer electrodes of the Bacon type rigidly attached to metal backing plates. The electrolyte and electrode materials are the same as those used in the porous diaphragm cell. The molten eutectic has a surface tension of 225 dynes/cm at 550°C and with this value the required pore sizes of the coarse- and fine-pored layer of the electrode are approximately 160 to 270 microns and 76 to 140 microns, respectively. This gives a working gas pressure range of 20 to 65 in. water gauge. Above this range the gas begins to bubble through the outer face of the electrode and below it the electrode is completely flooded and temporarily inactivated. The fuel activity is regained immediately when the pressure is raised above 20 in. water gauge and the electrolyte is forced back to the interface between the coarse and fine layers.

The two types of cell give very similar performances. The free electrolyte cell might be expected to have a lower internal resistance, but in practice the difference is not very marked because the fine-pore layers are always flooded and act in much the same way as porous diaphragms. The choice between the two types will depend ultimately on engineering design factors.

Performance Data

The usual range of operating temperatures of these cells is 550 to 700°C. With fuels such as hydrogen, carbon monoxide and methanol there is no activation or concentration polarization at current densities up to at least 140 amp/sq ft and the terminal voltage on load is determined primarily by the internal resistance of the cell. With methane, activation polarization is evident at temperatures below 600°C and the power output is between one-half and two-thirds of that obtained with hydrogen up to a current density of 20 amp/sq ft, above which value the output falls off rapidly. The situation is better at 700°C but there is still room for improvement of the catalytic activity of the anode with respect to methane.

Propane gives a better performance but there is a strong tendency to deposit carbon and block the gas passages. This is prevented by feeding water vapor with the fuel and the output is also improved.

Kerosene vapor at 650°C gives almost the same performance as hydrogen. Hitherto no difficulties have been experienced with this fuel.

Typical voltage-current density curves for a number of different cells and fuels are given in Figures 7-5 through 7-8. The large variations in internal resistances of the cells make it difficult to compare one curve with another directly, but in each case the curve obtained with hydrogen on the same cell is given. In all cases, the gas flow to the cell was such that at a current density of 50 amp/sq ft between 10 and 20 per cent of the fuel was consumed. The significance of this will appear later.

Diaphragm cells up to 5 in. diameter have been operated continuously and intermittently for periods up to 1000 hr, during which time no deterioration in performance has been observed. Life tests have always been terminated by such things as corrosion of the cell bodies or failure of sealing gaskets. The electrodes are quite stable and are not susceptible to poisoning.

With free-electrolyte cells, air electrodes are perfectly satisfactory but some trouble has been experienced with fuel electrodes due to insufficient mechanical strength and it has not yet been possible to carry out very prolonged life tests.

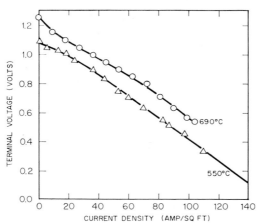

Figure 7-5. Voltage/current density curves hydrogen/air at atmospheric pressure 550°C and 690°C.

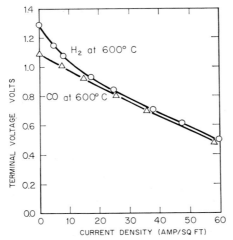

Figure 7-6. Voltage/current density curves hydrogen/air at atmospheric pressure, 600°C carbon monoxide at atmospheric pressure, 600°C.

Carbon Deposition

With all carbonaceous fuels there is potential danger of deposition of solid carbon in the cells causing blocking of gas passages and an inevitable loss of available energy due to an irreversible, non-electrochemical side reaction.

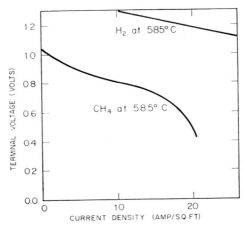

Figure 7-7. Voltage/current density curves hydrogen/air at atmospheric pressure, 585°C. Methane/air at atmospheric pressure, 585°C.

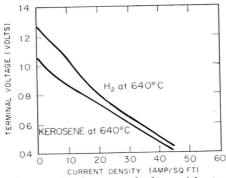

Figure 7-8. Voltage/current density curves hydrogen/air at atmospheric pressure, 640°C. Kerosene/air at atmospheric pressure, 640°C.

With pure carbon monoxide the Boudouard reaction can occur under certain conditions:

$$2CO = C + CO_2$$

Thermodynamic calculations show that at 600°C and a total gas pressure of 1 atm, carbon deposition is possible if the P_{CO_2}/P_{CO} ratio is less than 3 and at 700 and 800°C if this ratio is less than 0.7 and 0.2, respectively. Hence the trouble is more likely to occur at lower temperatures and with very pure carbon monoxide. Fortunately, this reaction is catalyzed specifically by iron oxides and reducible iron compounds and when these materials are not used in construction of the cell no trouble is experienced. This effectively eliminates iron oxide electrodes of the Davtyan type and also many iron alloys in the construction of cell bodies. Highly alloyed irons are satisfactory.

With hydrocarbon vapors carbon may be deposited by thermal cracking. This occurs with propane, for example, but not with methane or kerosene. It can be prevented by adding water vapor or carbon dioxide to the fuel gas.

Fuel Cell Efficiency

It is impossible to make a realistic assessment of the efficiency of a small single cell, partly for theoretical reasons which will appear shortly, and partly because of the practical difficulties of making small cells completely gas-tight. In any case a single cell can never be self-sufficient in heat and in order to maintain its temperature, it must be run inside a furnace which consumes more energy than the cell delivers. It is possible, however, to make a fair estimate of the efficiency of a battery based on data obtained with single cells and taking into account all the possible energy losses.

Cell efficiency can be expressed in one of four ways:

$$(1) \text{ Free energy efficiency} = \eta_F = \frac{\text{Electrical energy delivered to external circuit}}{(-\Delta F)} \times 100\%$$

$$(2) \text{ Thermal efficiency} = \eta_H = \frac{\text{Electrical energy delivered to external circuit}}{(-\Delta H)} \times 100\%$$

$$(3) \text{ Voltage efficiency} = \eta_V = \frac{\text{Observed terminal voltage}}{\text{Theoretical voltage}} \times 100\%$$

$$(4) \text{ Current efficiency} = \eta_C = \frac{\text{Observed current}}{\text{Current equivalent of gas consumed}} \times 100\%$$

ΔF and ΔH are the free energy and enthalpy changes in the over-all cell reaction.

η_F measures the efficiency of the cell as an energy converter. η_H may be used to compare the efficiency with that of a conventional generating process operating on a thermal cycle between the same initial and final states. Note that in a perfect fuel cell $\eta_F = 100$ per cent but the thermal efficiency may be greater or less than 100 per cent because of the relation $\Delta F = \Delta H -$

$T\Delta S$. When η_H is greater than 100 per cent the additional electrical energy is, of course, derived from the heat absorbed from the surroundings.

From the above definitions, $\eta_F = \eta_C \times \eta_V$. Such experimental evidence as is available suggests that in the absence of side reactions of the fuel, gas leaks or inter-electrode diffusion, and internal electrical leaks in the cell, $\eta_C = 100$ per cent. To a first approximation, then,

$$\eta_F = \frac{\text{Observed terminal voltage}}{\text{Theoretical voltage}}$$

The theoretical voltage of a cell operating on pure hydrogen and air is given by

$$E = E_0 - \frac{RT}{2F} \ln \frac{P^2_{H_2O}}{P^2_{H_2} \cdot P_{O_2}}$$

This value is to some extent indeterminate because, although we can put $P_{H_2} = 1$ atm and $P_{O_2} = 0.2$ atm, the value P_{H_2O} is small and unknown. This difficulty does not arise in cells with aqueous electrolyte where P_{H_2O} is fixed by the vapor pressure of the electrolyte. The same problem is present in a high temperature cell operating on carbon monoxide because P_{CO_2} in Equation (1) is not known, although it might be assumed to be fixed by the equilibrium pressure of carbon dioxide over the carbonate electrolyte. The chosen conditions for calculating the theoretical voltage are necessarily arbitrary, but since a perfect cell would be required to consume fuel at 1 atm pressure, oxygen at 0.2 atm and discharge the combustion product at 1 atm, a reasonable criterion is obtained by letting P_{H_2} or $P_{CO} = 1$ atm, $P_{O_2} = 0.2$ atm and P_{H_2O} or $P_{CO_2} = 1$ atm. We must recognize, however, the possibility of obtaining open-circuit voltages higher than the "theoretical" value defined in this way if very pure fuel gas, free from combustion products, is used. Very dry hydrogen, for example, gives voltages as high as 0.4 volt. higher than the "theoretical" value. This is partly due to the carbon dioxide concentration cell effect. With carbon monoxide, which is always likely to contain an appreciable amount of carbon dioxide, exceptionally high open-circuit voltages are not usually observed.

At a constant oxygen partial pressure, it is the ratio of the partial pressures of the combustion product and the fuel which determines the theoretical voltage. Clearly then, the accumulation of reaction products in the gas with the cell on load will reduce the output. It has been suggested that this can be overcome by partially reacting the gas and recycling it after removal of the combustion product by scrubbing or some other method. It is doubt-

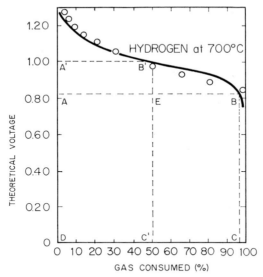

Figure 7-9. Theoretical voltage *vs.* per cent gas consumption. Solid line-theoretical points. ⊙-observed voltage +I.R. DROP. (Hydrogen at 700°C).

ful whether this would be economical. A better solution is to adopt multi-stage oxidation, as the following calculation shows.

Assume the cell to be fed with an excess of air so that the partial pressure of oxygen is substantially constant. Then in a steady state on load the theoretical cell voltage will be fixed by the ratio $P_{product}/P_{fuel}$. This value increases as the fuel passes from the inlet side of the electrode to the outlet side and one might expect that in the absence of polarization the observed terminal voltage would depend upon the outlet gas composition.

In Figure 7-9 the full line is a plot of theoretical voltage against percentage of gas consumed (i.e., outlet gas concentration) for a hydrogen-air cell at atmospheric pressure and 550°C. The points are experimental values of observed terminal voltage plus internal resistance drop obtained with a constant flow of pure dry hydrogen and varying current to give different percentage gas consumptions (the latter calculated from gas flow rate and Faraday's Law). The agreement is very satisfactory.

If 1 mole of fuel passes through the cell and 0.97 mole is consumed the outlet gas will contain 97 per cent water and 3 per cent hydrogen and the theoretical cell voltage will be given by point B in Figure 7-9. The energy output will be proportional to the area ABCD. If two cells are arranged in cascade, the outlet gas from the first passing to the second with the currents adjusted to consume 50 per cent of the hydrogen in the first cell and 47 per cent in the second, the two cells will have respectively voltages B' and B and total energy output will be proportional to the sum of the areas A'B'C'D and EBCC'. There is a net gain of A'B'EA. The maximum energy obtainable from 1 mole of gas is represented by the total area under the curve and this would be obtained from an infinite number of cells in cascade. Because of the rapid fall in voltage at high percentage conversions, there is nothing to be gained by trying to achieve more than about 97 per cent gas utilization. A single-stage oxidation, with 97 per cent gas utilization gives only 83 per cent of the available energy, whereas four-stage and eight-stage oxidation gives, respectively, 94 and 96 per cent. In practice, of course, the efficiency is lower than this because of ohmic polarization, but the same conclusion is valid, namely, that efficient conversion can be achieved only in a battery with a multi-stage arrangement of cells in cascade with respect to the gas flow.

It also follows from these considerations that voltage-current density curves for single cells are quite meaningless unless the percentage gas utilization is specified. This has been overlooked by all the earlier workers who either used very high gas supply rates and consumed a negligible proportion of the gas, or had no control of the gas supply and therefore no knowledge of the gas utilization. A complete description of the performance of a cell requires a set of voltage-current density curves at different levels of gas consumption. If it is desired to give a general indication of output with a single curve, the best level to choose is 50 per cent consumption.

Battery Efficiencies

A realistic assessment of the efficiency of a fuel battery taking into account all the probable energy losses can be made on the basis of the ideas developed in the previous paragraphs. This has been done for a battery with a nominal output of $2\frac{1}{2}$ kw at 50 volts.

The calculation is based on experimental results for single cells which give current densities of 50 amp/sq ft at terminal voltages of 0.8 volt at 50 per cent gas consumption with no activation or concentration polarization. This corresponds to an internal resistance of 0.004 ohm/sq ft of electrode area. Thus 64 cells in electrical series with 1 sq ft electrodes will give $2\frac{1}{2}$ kw output at 50 volts. The battery is divided into eight banks of eight cells each. In each bank the eight cells are parallel to the gas flow and the eight banks are fed in series. The total gas utilization is 97 per cent. By dividing the curve in Figure 7-9 into seven $12\frac{1}{2}$ per cent intervals and one $9\frac{1}{2}$ per cent interval, we can read the theoretical voltages for the cells of

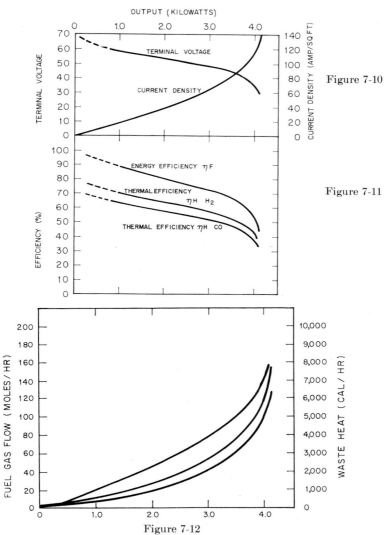

Figure 7-10

Figure 7-11

Figure 7-12

Figures 7-10, 7-11 and 7-12 show estimated performance curves for battery with nominal output of $2\frac{1}{2}$ kw at 50 volts.

each bank and then construct the current density-voltage curves for each bank. From these curves, we can derive the over-all efficiency of the battery. The results are summarized in Figures 7-10, 7-11 and 7-12, where terminal voltage, current density, efficiency and waste heat evolution are plotted against power output.

The output at which the battery becomes self-sustaining in temperature depends upon the efficiency of the lagging. It can be shown, for example, that a battery of this size with 3 in. of insulation having a K value of 0.06 Btu/(hr)(sq ft)(°F/ft) will be self-sustaining at outputs of more than 1.4 kw with carbon monoxide and 1.7 kw with hydrogen, the gas and air being fed cold. These limiting figures can be reduced by more efficient lagging and by preheating the gases using some of the waste heat. At higher outputs arrangements must be made for cooling the battery.

The present laboratory cells are $\frac{1}{2}$ in. thick. On this basis the output of the battery at its nominal rating of $2\frac{1}{2}$ kw would be 1 kw/cu ft of active volume (i.e., excluding thermal lagging) and 1.6 kw/cu ft at maximum output. The energy efficiencies at these two outputs are 78 and 50 per cent, respectively, and the thermal efficiencies would be about 60 per cent at $2\frac{1}{2}$ kw and 38 per cent at maximum output. Considerable improvements are expected from work now in hand to reduce the cell thickness and internal resistance.

Conclusions

Fuel cells of this type are capable of operating at high efficiency on air and a variety of carbonaceous fuel gases and vapors at atmospheric pressure in the temperature range 550 to 700°C. There is still room for improvement, but the present performance is considered to be sufficiently promising to warrant further large-scale development. The engineering design problems involved in constructing large self-sustaining batteries are well defined and there is no reason to suppose that any insurmountable difficulties will be encountered.

References

1. Davtyan, O. K., *Bull. Acad. Sci. U.R.S.S. Class. sci. tech.* 107, 125, (1946); E.R.A. Translation Ref. 1B. 884 (1949).
2. Greger, H. H., U. S. Patents 1,963,550 (1934); 2,175,523 (1939); 2,276,188 (1942).
3. Bacon, F., British Patent 667,298 (1952).
4. Allmand, A. J., and Ellingham, H. J. T., "Principles of Applied Electrochemistry," London, Longmans, 1924.

8. Nature of the Electrode Processes in Fuel Gas Cells

E. Gorin and H. L. Recht

Consolidation Coal Company
Research and Development Division
Library, Pennsylvania

Introduction

There has been considerable activity in recent years on fuel cell research. The work has encompassed many different types of cells. The major portion of the work, however, has been concentrated on the low[1] and medium temperature[2] hydrogen-oxygen cells and on the so-called high temperature gas cell.

No attempt will be made to review the rather voluminous literature in this field since many excellent review papers are available.[3]

The high temperature cell may arbitrarily be defined as a gas cell which operates at atmospheric pressure and at temperatures in the general range of 500 to 900°C. It operates either with hydrogen or mixtures of hydrogen and carbon monoxide as fuel gas and usually with air as the oxidant. This type of cell has created most interest as a potential source of Central Station power.

Work on the high temperature fuel cell is now under way at quite a few laboratories throughout the world. The most extensive and probably the most successful work has been carried out at the University of Amsterdam under the direction of J. A. A. Ketelaar[4]. Broers[5] in particular has recently published an extensive account of the work carried out at Amsterdam.

Work has been conducted until recently on the high temperature cell at the laboratories of the Consolidation Coal Company. Recent publications[6] have described some of the experimental results as well as methods that could be employed for effecting the integration of the cell operation with the gas manufacturing process. Such integration is essential to realize the potential advantage of the fuel cell in achieving a high efficiency for power generation.

The high temperature cell[7] utilized in this work has been similar in most respects to that used by Broers[5]. The electrolyte used was mixed alkali carbonates disposed on a specially prepared pure porous magnesia matrix. In addition to the metal gauzes used by Broers, porous sintered metals have been used as the fuel electrode and a semiconducting lithiated nickel oxide refractory as the air[8] electrode. Likewise, metal gauzes, and in particular nickel and silver, have been found to operate satisfactorily without the powdered metal activators used by Broers.

The basic problems that remain to be resolved before the fuel cell can attain commercial stature are the attainment of a system of acceptable life and power output. The resolution of these problems could be considerably expedited if a better understanding of the manner in which the cell functions were available.

The purpose of this chapter is to present some data in connection with the mechanism of the cell action. The experimental work carried out to date has not been sufficiently extensive to provide positive confirmation of the theories presented. The mechanism is described therefore without adequate experimental proof, in the hope that it may prove useful to other workers in the field.

Experimental Method and Results

The construction of the fuel cell, the method of fabrication of the components and the operating procedure have been described previously and will not be repeated here.[7] Likewise, some of the experimental results[6,7] have been presented before although in somewhat different form.

The data presented here serve as a basis for discussion of the mechanism of cell action. Most of the data revolve about the use of hydrogen as fuel gas. Considerable data have been accumulated also on carbon monoxide-carbon dioxide mixtures as fuel gas. The power outputs achieved are, in general, considerably lower than with hydrogen. These data are not included since the discussion revolves largely about the mechanism of the hydrogen and air electrodes.

It is felt that utilization of hydrogen will be the determining factor in any potential practical fuel cell system. All fuel gases that would be utilized in practice would be rich in hydrogen. Due to the relatively poor performance of the carbon monoxide electrode, the major portion of the carbon monoxide would likely be utilized indirectly through conversion *in situ* to hydrogen by means of the water gas shift reaction. The major distinction in practice between low-temperature and high-temperature cells would be the ability of the latter to utilize the carbon monoxide even if it is only indirectly as discussed above.

Tables 8-1A and 8-1B summarize the operating data obtained with the carbonate type cell.

The electrolyte employed in the work reported here was an equimolar mixture of sodium and lithium carbonates throughout. Carbon dioxide was always added to the air stream as a depolarizer. The amount used is specified in Table 8-1A.

The results given in the table are, except for individual cases noted, smoothed results. The method of least squares was used for this purpose, based on the assumption of a linear drop in cell voltage with current drain. In order to apply this method it was necessary to correct for the decrease in open-circuit voltage due to change in gas composition as a result of accumulation of reaction products with current drain. The theoretical voltage was calculated by application of the Nernst equation. This figure is given in Column 4 of Table 8-1B. It is noted that the theoretical voltage with no current drain could not be calculated since it is affected by the very small but unknown amount of carbon dioxide in the hydrogen fuel gas.

TABLE 8-1A. SUMMARY FUEL CELL PERFORMANCE DATA
A. CONDITIONS OF RUNS

Run No.	Temp., °C	Fuel Electrode	Air Electrode	Fuel Gas Composition	% CO_2 in Air
Ag-2a	700	"D" porosity porous nickel	80-mesh silver gauze	97% H_2–3% H_2O	16.6
Ag-2b	750	"D" porosity porous nickel	80-mesh silver gauze	97% H_2–3% H_2O	11.1
Ag-2c	800	"D" porosity porous nickel	80-mesh silver gauze	97% H_2–3% H_2O	18.2
Ag-12	750	"D" porosity porous nickel	80-mesh silver gauze	97% H_2–3% H_2O	11.1
Ag-13	800	Fe powder on "D" porosity stainless steel	80-mesh silver gauze	97% H_2–3% H_2O	11.1
N-6	700	"D" porosity porous nickel	Lithiated nickel oxide	97% H_2–3% H_2O	11.1
N-16	750	"D" porosity porous nickel	Lithiated nickel oxide	97% H_2–3% H_2O	11.1
Ag-7B	825	80-mesh silver gauze	80-mesh silver gauze	97% H_2–3% H_2O	16.6
Ag-7C	825	80-mesh silver gauze	80-mesh silver gauze	2 CO–1 CO_2	16.6

TABLE 8-1B. SUMMARY FUEL CELL PERFORMANCE DATA
B. CURRENT DRAIN BEHAVIOR

Run No.	Current Density ma/cm²	Voltage		Specific Resistance, ohm cm	
		Measured	Calc. Open Circuit	Measured	Calculated
Ag-2a	0	1.216	—	6.4	9.1
	30	0.918	1.191	↓	↓
	65	0.578	1.170		
Ag-2b	0	1.250	—	5.2	5.3
	30	1.012	1.180		
	65	0.781	1.128		
	100	0.572	1.100		
	127	0.426	1.076	↓	↓
Ag-2c	0	1.170	—	7.6	—
	65	0.625	1.191		—
	100	0.418	1.160	↓	—
Ag-12	0	1.180	—	7.4	—
	35	.923	1.184		—
	65	.680	1.145	↓	—
Ag-13	0	1.143	—	4.2	—
	32*	0.832	1.206	↓	—
Ag-7B	0	1.090	—	3.9	—
	28*	0.897	—		—
	57*	0.758	—	↓	—
Ag-7C	0	0.181	0.931	—	—
	11*	0.140	—	—	—
N-6	0	1.230	—	7.3	11.1
	30	0.872	1.212		
	65	0.440	1.165		
	100	0.030	1.138	↓	↓
N-16	0	1.120	—	3.4	—
	62*	0.569	—	↓	—

* Actual experimental points.

Application of the statistical method to the treatment of the results is illustrated in Figures 8-1 and 8-2. The dotted lines present the field in which the experimental data should fall within a confidence limit of 95 per cent. The fit suggests that the cell operates without substantial electrode polarization at 700 to 750°C with porous nickel fuel electrode and either silver gauze or lithiated nickel oxide as the air electrode.

The above statement must be qualified, however, by the area as shown for the confidence limits. Polarization up to .06 volt is permitted at 750°C and up to .08 volt at 700°C.

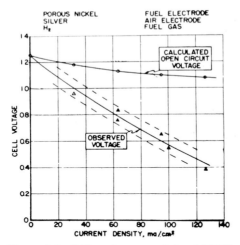

Figure 8–1. Cell performance data at 750°C.

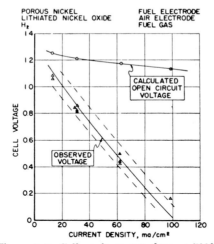

Figure 8–2. Cell performance data at 700°C.

Another check for polarization is the agreement between cell resistance as measured directly by an a.c. bridge and that determined by the least squares analysis. The agreement is excellent for Run Ag-2b at 750°C. Broer,[5] likewise, reports excellent agreement between calculated and measured resistance even at lower temperatures. In the 700°C runs, however, the calculated resistance is definitely higher than measured. This does not necessarily indicate activation polarization, however, as will be shown later.

No realistic comparison could be made between measured and calculated resistance in many of the runs shown. This is because the open-circuit voltage falls in some cases below the theoretical value. This is attributed to limited mixing of the fuel gas and air through microscopic cracks in the electrolyte matrix. Such cracks were observed after the runs were completed.

A few other interesting observations can be made. Silver is found to be a fair hydrogen electrode although not nearly as good as nickel. It is practically worthless, however, as a carbon monoxide electrode. Iron does not appear to be as good a hydrogen electrode as nickel. The data presented are not conclusive on this point. Numerous other data, not presented here, all point, however, to the same conclusions.

The above discussion is generally in accord with the findings of Broers.[5]

Internal Resistance of the Cell

The high internal resistance of the cell during operation is noteworthy. Separate conductivity measurements were made to determine whether this could be attributed to some peculiar property of the electrolyte matrix. Measurements were made with the matrix loaded with an excess of the mixed carbonate melt. Two flat silver gaskets were used as electrodes. An average value of the resistance/cm^2 of 0.7 ohm was found in the temperature range of 700 to 800°C. The expected value from the thickness and porosity of the matrix, 0.2 cm and 28 per cent, respectively, and the specific conductivity of the melt 2.9 ohm^{-1} cm is only 0.25 ohm. Even so, the measured value is smaller by a factor of 7 to 10 than that observed during cell operation. Broers also found a similar high resistance during cell operation.

The high ratio between the resistance measured during cell operation and the inherent resistivity of the electrolyte matrix can be taken to have the following significance. The melt inventory must be adjusted until a small area of contact is maintained between the electrode and the electrolyte. This may be required to maintain proper access of the gas to the electrode surface, and greatly increases the effective resistance of the electrolyte if the contact area is sufficiently small.

Consider, for example, an idealized model where the electrode maintains symmetrical square areas of contact having individual areas Δ^2 and a spacing between contact area d as shown in Figure 8-3.

The effective resistance of a cell containing two such identical infinite plane square mesh electrodes separated by an electrolyte of thickness l may be calculated by a solution of Laplace's equation which relates the potential V to the position in the electrolyte

$$\Delta^2 V = 0$$

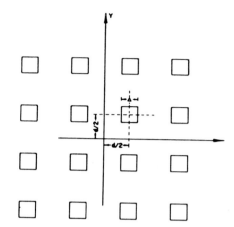

Figure 8–3. Diagram of square mesh electrode.

The calculation desired is the potential drop across such an electrode system as a function of the current density $\bar{\imath}$ and the specific resistance $\bar{R}$. This can then be compared with the potential drop across plane flat electrodes. The appropriate boundary conditions and solution of the above partial differential equation for this particular case has been given previously[6b] and is omitted here for the sake of brevity. The solution is shown graphically in Figure 8-4 where the ratio R_{eff}/R is plotted as a function of l/d with Δ/d as a parameter. R_{eff}/R is the ratio of the effective resistance to the resistance obtaining in the case where one has plane flat electrodes.

It is noted, for example, that the experimentally observed ratio R_{eff}/R of about 8.0 could be explained if the spacing d is about 3.2×10^{-2} cm, i.e., *the space between wire junctions in the screen electrode used,* and $\Delta d = 1.8 \times 10^{-2}$. The above corresponds to an l/d ratio of 6.3 which is in accord with the electrolyte thickness of 2 mm used in our work. It is interesting to note that such a situation corresponds to confining the electrode reaction to only 3.2×10^{-4} cm^2/sq cm of electrolyte surface.

The effective resistance ratio is very much a function of the spacing between contact areas. It is clear from Figure 8-4 that the resistance drops markedly for constant fractional active area as the spacing decreases. The importance of this factor in optimizing cell design is obvious.

Another way of illustrating this point is to repeat the same calculation with a different geometrical pattern. This was done with a parallel wire type electrode as shown in Figure 8-5. Such a system would correspond to

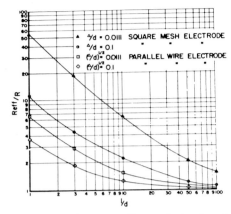

Figure 8–4. Effective resistance ratio *vs.* electrode contact pattern.

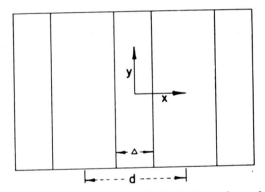

Figure 8–5. Diagram of parallel wire-type electrode.

the "hypothetical" case of a wire gauze electrode where none of the cross wires made contact.

Laplace's equation for this case was solved with the following pertinent boundary conditions:

$$\frac{\partial V}{\partial Z} = \frac{i\bar{R}}{\Delta/d} \qquad \text{for } x = -\Delta/2 \text{ to } + \Delta/2$$

$$= 0 \qquad \text{for } x = -d/2 \text{ to } -\Delta/2$$

$$\text{and } x = \Delta/2 \text{ to } d/2$$

It was assumed again for simplicity that both electrodes were identical. The solution is

$$V = V_0 + \frac{i\bar{R}l}{2} + \sum_{n=1}^{\infty} \frac{i\bar{R}d}{\pi^2 n^2 r} \sin(n\pi r) \tan k \left(\frac{n\pi l}{d}\right) \qquad \text{at } Z = l/2 \quad (1)$$

$$\frac{R_{\text{eff}}}{R} = \frac{V_{z=l/2} - V_{z=l/2}}{i\bar{R}l} = 1 + \frac{2}{\pi^2 \left(\frac{l}{d}\right) r} \sum_{n=1}^{\infty} \frac{\sin n\pi r}{n^2} \tan k \left(\frac{n\pi l}{d}\right) \quad (2)$$

where $r = \Delta/d$ and $\bar{R}$ is the specific resistance.

The fractional area covered in this case is Δ/d as against $(\Delta/d)^2$ for the square mesh electrode. The points therefore were plotted with this in mind such that $(\Delta/d)^{1/2}$ for the parallel wire type electrode corresponded to Δ/d for the square mesh type.

It is readily seen that the parallel wire type electrode can tolerate a much smaller contact area without a large increase in cell resistance. Again the desirability of maintaining close spacing between contact points in cell design is emphasized.

Since the actual area of contact during operation of the cell was unknown, one cannot state definitely that this is the major cause of the high resistance observed. Rather, it seems likely that the low melt inventory itself may be partly responsible by causing part of the electrolytic conduction to be effected through small zones of extremely thin layers of melt.

As will be shown later, however, it is possible in principle to have a relatively low resistance as measured with an a.c. bridge and an effectively high resistance during cell operation as a result of the electrode reaction being concentrated in a very small area.

Maximum Rate of Electrode Reaction

The electrode reaction as mentioned above must be concentrated in a very small area due to the difficulty of providing for access of the gas through the three-phase limit where electrode, electrolyte, and gas meet. The minimum area required may be estimated as follows. The electrode reaction can certainly not take place, in the limit, any faster than gas molecules striking the metal surface can be adsorbed. Fortunately, Eyring[9] has provided us with a method for estimating this rate using his theory of absolute reaction rates. For the case where gas molecules strike a surface to form an immobile dissociated adsorbed film, Eyring gives the equation

$$v_1 = \frac{1}{2} sc_g c_s \frac{\sigma}{\sigma_F} \frac{h^4}{8\pi^2 I (2\pi mkT)^{3/2}} e^{-E_1/RT} \quad (3)$$

where v_1 is that rate of adsorption in molecules/cm^2 sec and E_1 is the activation energy of adsorption. If we use $s = 4$ and $C_s = 10^{15}$ sites/cm^2 as suggested by Eyring one calculates the adsorption rate for hydrogen as

$$v_1 = 2.29 \times 10^{-5} \Gamma^{3/2} P_{mm} e^{-E_1/RT} \text{ mole/cm}^2 \text{sec} \qquad (4)$$

Thus, if E_1 is small, i.e., equal to 3000 cal/mole, the endothermic heat of solution in nickel, the rate can be as large as 130 mole/cm^2 sec at 750°C. The above rate is sufficiently large such that a current density of 100 ma/cm^2 could be achieved on a surface as small as 4.0×10^{-9} cm^2/cm^2 of electrolyte area. Such a concentration of the electrode reaction, however, would, in view of the preceding considerations, cause a very considerable increase in the effective resistance of the cell.

Under comparable assumptions, the maximum rate of the electrode reaction of the air electrode would be somewhat smaller due to the lower partial pressure and the higher molecular weight and moment of inertia of oxygen. Even so, a rate of the order of 1 mole/cm^2 sec is possible in this case.

The Three-Phase Limit

It is obvious that some mechanism must be in force for broadening of the three-phase limit. Otherwise two deleterious factors come strongly into play, i.e., activation polarization as a result of concentrating the electrode reaction on a very small area and the concomitant high effective resistance discussed above.

Three mechanisms may be cited: (1) diffusion of the gas through a thin film in the neighborhood of the interface; (2) permeation of gas through the bulk electrode metal, and (3) surface diffusion across the electrode surface.

The first seems unlikely even though data on the permeation of gases through salt melts at high temperatures are unavailable.

Some data are available, however, on the diffusion and permeability rates of hydrogen and oxygen through aqueous solutions of electrolytes. For example, the diffusion constant of hydrogen through 20 per cent NaOH solution[10] is reported as about 10^{-5} cm^2/sec at 25°C. The solubility C_0 is of the order of 2×10^{-7} mole/cc at atmospheric pressure. The rate of transport of hydrogen to the electrode surface per unit area through an electrolyte film of thickness d is thus

$$\frac{D(C_0 - C_1)}{d} = \frac{i}{2 \times 96500}$$

where C_1 is the concentration at the electrode interface. The exposure of as much as 1 cm^2 of surface to a thin film of electrolyte per cm^2 of electrolyte area seems rather unlikely with electrodes of the type used in this work. Even so one calculates in the above case that the average thickness of electrolyte film would have to be less than 6×10^{-6} cm to maintain a current density of 100 ma/cm^2.

Corresponding data are absent, of course, under conditions where the high temperature cell operates, but it is not likely that the permeability of gases through salt melts would be any higher due to a probably very low solubility of gases in melts. It would be interesting of course to obtain such data.

Data are available, however, from which the rate of permeation of gases through metals can be calculated. Probably the best data on the solubility of hydrogen in nickel and iron are those of Armbruster.[11] Edwards[12] gives corresponding data on the diffusion constant of hydrogen in nickel. Combining the two sets of data, one finds the permeation rate of hydrogen through nickel at atmospheric pressure $P = DC_0 = 1.46 \times 10^{-6} e^{-13100/RT}$ mole/cm^7 sec. The permeation rate at 750°C is thus 2.37×10^{-9} mole/cm^2 sec/cm or greater by a factor of 10^3 than the permeation of hydrogen through electrolyte solutions at room temperature.

The rest of this chapter is concerned with an examination of the permeation of gases through metal electrodes as a mechanism for broadening the three-phase limit. Some consideration is given also to the last mechanism.

Permeable Metal Gas Electrodes

A simplified model of the metal electrolyte contact can be set up such that the problem of a permeable metal electrode reaction can be treated mathematically. Such an idealized model is represented graphically in Figure 8-6. Here a cross section of the contact between the electrode and electrolyte matrix is represented. The cross section represents either a spherical metal granule of radius r of the porous metal electrode, or of a cylindrical wire of the same radius, where a wire gauze electrode is used. The angle ψ represents the portion of the cross section where contact is maintained between the electrolyte and the metal electrode surface.

It is now necessary to make assumptions relative to the rate controlling processes. These must be made primarily on a basis of "reasonableness." It is assumed, therefore that the rate of solution of gas into the metal is controlled by the rate of penetration of the gas from an adsorbed layer of dissociated atoms. Similarly, the rate of dissolution is controlled by the rate at which the gas penetrates the metal surface to form the same adsorbed layer.

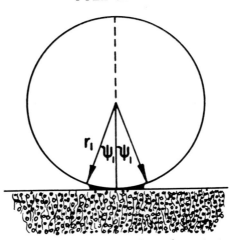

Figure 8-6. Diagram of electrode contact.

Experimentally, it is known that the rate of solution and dissolution of gas in metals is very rapid relative to the rate of permeation through the metal bulk.[12] No information is available therefore on the rate determining step for adsorption and desorption. The experimental facts are also consistent with the hypothesis that the dissolved gases are present in dissociated form when dissolved in metals. The adsorbed layer may therefore also be considered as being present in dissociated form.

Two further assumptions are now required, namely, that the rate of adsorption is very rapid relative to the rate of solution such that the concentration in the adsorbed layer is in equilibrium with gas phase. Similarly, it is assumed that the electrode reaction involves the adsorbed layer and again this is very rapid relative to the rate of desorption from the metal bulk. Thus again, the equilibrium electrode potential is maintained as determined by the concentration in the adsorbed layer.

Since the electrode must be at constant potential, it follows that the concentration of the adsorbed layer must be constant at all points within the electrolyte. This concentration C_1 may be considered to be equivalent to that in equilibrium with gas at a pressure P_1 in atmosphere, i.e., $C_1 = C_0\sqrt{P_1}$. Similarly, the concentration of the adsorbed layer in the area outside of the electrolyte C_g, must be constant and in equilibrium with pressure of gas existing in the gas phase, i.e., $C_g = C_0\sqrt{P_g}$. C_0 is the concentration in equilibrium with 1 atm of gas.

The rate of permeation of the gas through the electrode may be obtained by solution of Fick's diffusion equation. For steady flow, this reduces to

$$D\nabla^2 C = 0 \qquad (5)$$

The boundary conditions for solution of Equation (5) based on the above assumptions are:

$$D\left(\frac{\partial C}{\partial r}\right)_{r=r_1} = -k(C - C_1) \qquad \psi = 0 \text{ to } \psi_1$$

$$D\left(\frac{\partial C}{\partial r}\right)_{r=r_1} = +k(C_g - C) \qquad \psi = \psi_1 \text{ to } \pi$$

where k is the rate of desorption of the gas from solution in the metal and C is the concentration of gas in the metal.

Two solutions are obtained for the two cases considered:

(1) *Spherical Electrode Contact:*

$$C = \frac{(C_g + C_1) + (C_g - C_1)h}{2}$$

$$- \left(\frac{k}{2D}\right)(C_g - C_1)\sum_{m=1}^{\infty} \frac{r^m[P_{m-1}(h) - P_{m+1}(h)]P_m(x)}{r_1^{m-1}\left(m + \frac{kr_1}{D}\right)} \quad (6)$$

where $x = \cos\psi$, $h = \cos\psi_1$, and $P_m(x)$ are the Legendre polynomials of the first kind.

$$F = \pi r_1 D(C_g - C_1)X_1 \tag{7}$$

where

$$X_1 = \left(\frac{kr_1}{D}\right)\sum_{m=1}^{\infty} \frac{m[P_{m-1}(h) - P_{m+1}(h)]^2}{(2m + 1)\left(m + \frac{kr_1}{D}\right)} \tag{8}$$

The flux F above is the total flow of gas through the metal electrode surface and is obtained by the integration

$$F = -2\pi r_1^2 D \int_{\psi_1}^{\pi} \left(\frac{\partial C}{\partial r}\right)_{r=r_1} \sin\psi \, d\psi \tag{9}$$

Now the flux F must equal the current flow so that we obtain

$$N\pi r_1 P \sqrt{P_g}\left(1 - \sqrt{\frac{P_1}{P_g}}\right)X_1 = \frac{i}{96500n} \tag{10}$$

where i is the current density in amp/cm^2, N is the number of spheres making contact/cm^2 area, n is the number of electrons involved in the electrode process (2 in the case of hydrogen) and $P = DC_0$ is the permeability of the gas through the metal. The above equation may be used to calculate the extent of electrode polarization ΔE as determined by the slow permeation through the electrode

$$\Delta E = \frac{RT}{nF} \ln \left(\frac{P_1}{P_g}\right) \tag{11}$$

The maximum current that may be drawn is determined by the value of i in Equation (10) when $P_1 = 0$.

The basic assumption in the above derivation is that activation polarization is absent, i.e., the electrode reaction is very rapid. It will be seen in what follows that a rapid electrode reaction is a necessity in order to obtain adequate permeation rates in any case.

An interesting feature of Equation (10) is that the permeation rate decreases only as the square root of the pressure. This feature tends to favor this mechanism of broadening the three-phase limit in the low pressure range. The extent of polarization is thus proportional to permeation rate of the electrode P and is, as will be seen later, relatively insensitive to the rate of the electrode process.

(2) *Cylindrical Wire Electrode Contact:*

The solutions of Equation (5) are obtained in this case in exactly the same fashion as before. They are given below

$$C = C_g - \frac{\psi_1}{\pi}(C_g - C_1)$$
$$- \frac{2}{\pi}\left(\frac{k}{D}\right)(C_g - C_1)\sum_{n=1}^{\infty} \frac{r^n \sin\psi_1 \cos n\psi}{r_1^{n-1} n\left(n + \frac{kr_1}{D}\right)} \tag{12}$$

$$F = D(C_g - C_1)\left(\frac{kr_1}{D}\right)\left(\frac{4}{\pi}\right)\sum_{n=1}^{\infty} \frac{\sin^2\psi_1}{n(n + kr_1/D)} \tag{13}$$

$$NP\sqrt{P_g}\left(1 - \sqrt{\frac{P_1}{P_g}}\right)X_2 = \frac{i}{96500n} \tag{14}$$

$$X_2 = \frac{4}{\pi}\left(\frac{kr_1}{D}\right)\sum_{n=1}^{\infty} \frac{\sin^2\psi_1}{n\left(n + \frac{kr_1}{D}\right)} \tag{15}$$

Equations (12)–(15) are very similar to the spherical case. N in this case is defined as the number of cylindrical wires of unit length in contact with 1 cm^2 of electrolyte surface.

It is noted that in all cases the flux factor X in the above equations is determined only by the term (kr_1/D). The rate constant for the electrode reaction k is unknown.

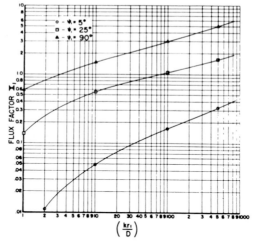

Figure 8-7. Flux factor *vs.* X_1 for spherical electrode.

However, it is possible to make some deductions from the experimental data as to the permissible range of this rate. It is implicit in the above derivation that the rate of the electrode process $k(C_g - C_1)$ must be less than the rate of adsorption from the gas phase.

Now consider porous nickel as a hydrogen electrode. It was shown previously that a maximum value for the adsorption rate at 750°C is of the order of 130 mole/cm^2 sec. For hydrogen in nickel, $D = 6 \times 10^{-5}$ cm^2 sec^{-1} and $C_0 = 3 \times 10^{-5}$ mole/cc at 750°C. Thus for a particle 65 microns in diameter (the mean particle size of the metal granules in the electrode used)

$$k(C_0) < 130 \qquad \frac{kr_1}{D} < 2 \times 10^8$$

It is therefore clear that for the present very large values of (kr_1/D) are not ruled out. Computations of the flux factor X, however, become very laborious for values of $(kr_1/D) > 500$. Computed values of the flux factor as a function of the contact angle ψ_1 and the flux factor are shown in Figure 8-7. It may be shown from the behavior of Equation (8) that as kr_1/D increases indefinitely so does the flux factor. It is seen from Figure 8-7 that X may be extrapolated to higher values of (kr_1/D) by use of the empirical relationship

$$X_1 = A \left(\frac{kr_1}{D}\right)^n$$

The polarization curves calculated in this way for several assigned values of (kr_1/D) and for several immersion angles are illustrated in Figure 8-8. The cases shown correspond to perfect contact between the electrode and electrolyte, i.e., every granule in a close-packed array makes contact.

It may be noted that the polarization curves are readily translated to different values of P, N, r, and X. Thus, the current density at which an equivalent polarization is obtained is proportional to P, N and X. For close-packed array of contacts it is inversely proportional to r_1. For the same number of contacts/cm² it is proportional to r_1.

The experimental results with the hydrogen nickel electrode showed that the polarization voltage was less than .08 volt at temperatures above 700°C. It is seen from Figure 8-8 that such a result can reasonably be achieved with the permeation mechanism cited although the case is far from proven.

The permeation rate, as noted above, goes down with temperature. Thus at 600°C it is lower by a factor of 3 and consequently only ⅓ as much current could be drawn before an equivalent amount of polarization sets in. The earlier onset of polarization at lower operating temperatures has been noted in our work and by others.

The polarization curves shown in Figure 8-8 correspond to rather perfect contact between electrode and electrolyte. The effective resistance ratio may be estimated as discussed above. Take for example, the case shown for $\psi = 5°$, the values of Δ/d, and l/d in this case are .02 and 30, respectively. Referring to Figure 8-4 the calculated $R_{eff}/R = 2.5$ which is considerably smaller than the observed value of 7. In actuality, less than perfect contact may be anticipated. The case is also illustrated in Figure 8-8 where only one in two particles at the electrode surface actually make

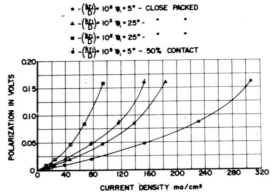

Figure 8–8. Polarization curves for H_2 spherical electrode.

contact. The predicted polarization in this case is in accord with that observed while R_{eff}/R rises according to Figure 8-4 to 3.5 which is closer to the observed ratio.

One must make one important qualification, however, since it can be shown that for high values of (kr_1/D) the current is concentrated over a relatively small fraction of the total contact area. Thus the effective resistance ratio would actually be greater than the value estimated above.

As a matter of fact, a peculiar feature of this treatment of the electrode process is that an extremely rapid electrode reaction causes it to be concentrated in a small area and thus increases the effective internal resistance of the cell. This provides a mechanism for explaining the observed situation where the effective internal resistance of the cell during operation is greater than that measured with the a.c. bridge and where activation polarization is absent.

The iron electrode may be evaluated in a similar fashion. The permeability of hydrogen through iron, taken from data of Smithells and Ramsley,[13] may be described by the following equation

$$P_0 = 2.01 \times 10^{-7} \, e^{-9600/RT} \, \text{mole/cm}^2 \, \text{sec/cm}.$$

Thus, P_0 at 750°C is equal to 1.8×10^{-9} which is very close to the value for the permeability of nickel. On this basis its performance as a hydrogen electrode should be very similar to nickel which is in accord with the facts.

The relatively poor performance of the carbon monoxide electrode may be ascribed to its low permeability through the metal electrodes.

We will now turn our attention to a discussion of the silver electrode. This electrode was used both as a hydrogen and air electrode in the form of wire gauze. We therefore use Equation (15) to discuss this case. The variation of the flux factor X with (kr_1/D) using the contact angle as parameter is shown in Figure 8-9. Again the flux factor may be extrapolated to higher values of (kr_1/D) by means of the empirical equation

$$X_2 = A \left(\frac{kr_1}{D} \right)^n$$

The justification again is the behavior of Equation (15) which shows that X increases indefinitely as (kr_1/D) increases. As a matter of fact it may be shown that Equation (15) takes the form

$$X_2 = \frac{4}{\pi} \sum_{n=1}^{\infty} \frac{\sin^2 \psi_1}{n}$$

as $(kr_1/D) \to \infty$. The above series diverges and thus X_2 becomes infinite.

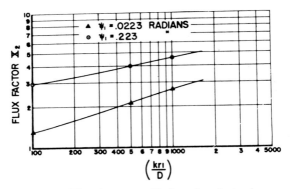

Figure 8–9. Flux factor *vs.* X_1 for wire electrode.

Likewise it may be shown that the current is concentrated in an infinitely small area.

The permeability of oxygen through silver was measured by Johnson and LaRose. Their results may be expressed by the equation

$$P_0 = 6.2 \times 10^{-6} \, e^{-22600/RT}$$

and shows a value for P_0 of 9.3×10^{-11} mole/cm^2 sec at 750°C. The diffusion coefficient may be obtained by combining the solubility data of Steacie and Johnson[15] with the above permeability data. Thus the value of D at 750°C is 9.5×10^{-6} cm^2 sec^{-1}. By the same argument as was developed previously for nickel, we find that the maximum possible value of $kr_1/D \cong 7 \times 10^7$. The maximum current that can be drawn in air under the assumption that all wires contact the electrolyte matrix throughout their length can now be computed for various assigned values of (kr_1/D). These figures are shown in Table 8-2. It is now seen that permeation through a silver air electrode is nowhere sufficiently fast to explain its performance.

Similar considerations may be made with regard to the silver hydrogen electrode. Accurate data are not available for the permeation rate of hy-

TABLE 8-2. SHORT-CIRCUIT CURRENT FOR 80-MESH SILVER
WIRE GAUZE ELECTRODE $r_1 = 7 \times 10^3$ CM

Contact Angle	kr_1/D	Short-Circuit Current ma/cm^2
12.8°	2000	5.0
1.28°	2000	2.8
1.28°	7×10^7	42.0

drogen through silver. The indications again are, however, that it would be insufficient to explain its performance as a hydrogen electrode.

To resolve these discrepancies, it is necessary to assume that the permeation rate through a thin surface layer of the metal is much greater than that through the metal in bulk. Equations may be derived for this case in a manner similar to the bulk permeation case treated above. The result, for example, for rapid permeation through a thin surface spherical shell of thickness Δ is given below

$$F = \pi r_1 D (C_g - C_1) X_3 \qquad (17)$$

$$X_3 = \left(\frac{kr_1}{D}\right) \sum_{m=1}^{\infty} \frac{m[P_{m-1}(h) - P_{m+1}(h)]^2}{(2m + 1)\left(m + \dfrac{kr_1^2}{\Delta D(m + 1)}\right)} \qquad (18)$$

Thus, the form of Equation (18) is identical to that for bulk diffusion, the only change being in the flux factor X_3. The dependence of the polarization voltage on the system variables is thus identical.

In conclusion, the performance of nickel and iron electrodes can be explained on the basis of the bulk permeation rate through the metal. The silver electrode performance required the introduction of the concept of accelerated surface diffusion. Further experimental data are required to determine whether variation of cell performance with system variables such as gas concentration behaves in the predicted fashion.

References

1. Evans, G. E., Proceedings of the 12th Annual Battery Research and Development Conference (U. S. Army Signal Corps Research and Development Laboratories Publication) May 1958.
2. Bacon, F. T., *Beama J.*, **61**, 2–8 (1954).
3. McKee, J. H., "The Production of Electricity From Coal," *British Coal Utilization Research Assoc. Bull.*, **9**, No. 7, 193–200 (1945).
   Adams, A. M., Fuel Cells II; Low Temperature Cells, Future Development, *Chem. & Process Eng.*, **35**, 238–240, 1954.
4. Ketelaar, J. A. A., *Die Ingenieur*, **66**, 34 E 88–91 (August 20, 1954).
5. Broers, G. H. J., "High Temperature Galvanic Cells," Thesis, University of Amsterdam, 1958.
6. Gorin, E., and Recht, H. L., a. *Mech. Eng.*, **81**, No. 3, 63 (1959); b. *Chem. Eng. Progr.*, in press.
7. Gorin, E., and Recht, H. L., Proceedings of the Tenth Annual Battery Conference, May, 1956; Proceedings of the Twelfth Annual Battery Conference, May, 1958; Quarterly Reports 1–17 to the Signal Corps Engineering Laboratories, Fort Monmouth, New Jersey, 1954–1958.
8. Gorin, E., and Recht, H. L., U. S. Patent 2,914,596, November, 1959.

9. Eyring, H., Glasstone, S., and Laidler, K. J., "Theory of Rate Process" New York, McGraw-Hill Book Co., 1941.
10. Ipatieff, V., and Tikhomirov, V. I., *J. Gen. Chem. USSR*, **7**, 736–9 (1931).
11. Armbruster, M., *J. Am. Chem. Soc.*, **65**, 1050 (1943).
12. Edwards, A. G., *Brit. J. Appl. Phys.*, **8**, 406 (1957).
13. Smithells, C. J., and Ramsley, C. B., *Proc. Roy. Soc. London*, **A, 157**, 292 (1936).
14. Johnson, F., and LaRose, P., *J. Am. Chem. Soc.*, **46**, 1377 (1924).
15. Steacie and Johnson, *Proc. Roy. Soc.*, **A, 112**, 542 (1926).

9. Molten Alkali Carbonate Cells With Gas-Diffusion Electrodes

DAVID L. DOUGLAS

General Electric Company
Research Laboratory
Schenectady, New York

Early work in the General Electric Research Laboratory on high temperature fuel cells,[1] paralleling that in other laboratories,[2] included the fabrication of Davtyan cells and led to the elucidation of the nature of the "solid" electrolyte. From this followed an appreciation of the molten alkali carbonate electrolyte. A brief study of the ternary system consisting of lithium, sodium and potassium carbonates revealed that certain mixtures become molten at about 400°C and are stable to above 800°C. At this point an investigation of the behavior of electrodes of the gas-diffusion type was initiated. The use of a free liquid electrolyte—without the retaining ceramic matrix usual in studies of high temperature fuel cells—offered the possibility of studying the behavior of individual electrodes by means of a reference electrode. This chapter reports the results of a preliminary investigation of gas-diffusion electrodes in molten alkali carbonate electrolyte.

Experimental

The apparatus, shown in Figure 9-1, was designed for convenience in testing electrode designs and materials. No attempts were made to obtain significant power output nor to determine the operating life of the cell assemblies. Figure 9-1 shows a particular assembly consisting of a carbon monoxide electrode, an oxygen electrode, a reference electrode and a thermocouple immersed in a crucible of molten alkali carbonates. Gold was selected as a crucible material by virtue of its being the only material *completely* unattacked by the very corrosive melt. "Teflon" was used as a packing in the glands, and rubber O-rings served as gas-seals in the adapters on the upper ends of the electrode tubes.

Fuel and oxidant gases were supplied from the panel shown in Figure 9-2. This permitted control of flow rates from 1 to 15 cu cm/min. The meter-

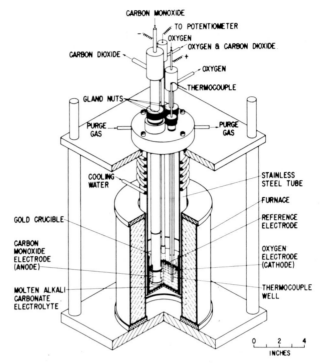

Figure 9–1. Fuel cell assembly.

ing valves could be readily adjusted to maintain any pressure in the electrodes from 0.5 to 10 psig over the entire range of flow rates.

Gas-diffusion electrodes consisted of porous metal bodies attached to alumina tubes. The porous materials were those commercially available, with
the exception of silver. Porous silver structures were made in the laboratory
by sintering appropriate powders in graphite molds at about 700°C. No
great efforts at selecting or controlling pore size distribution have been
made as yet. Table 9-1 lists the porous metals used and the porosity, pore
diameters and specific areas of each. A further indication of the pore structures is given in Figure 9-3. No attempt was made to develop structures
containing the networks of micro-pores (10 to 100Å diameters), which have
proved successful in yielding high current densities in gas-diffusion electrodes for low temperature cells. Such micro-pores may be expected to sinter
out rapidly at elevated temperatures.

The detailed construction of the type of electrode used in the majority

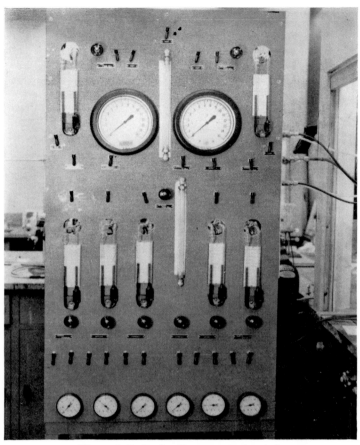

Figure 9-2. Fuel cell gas control panel.

TABLE 9-1. POROSITY, PORE-SIZE AND SPECIFIC AREA
OF ELECTRODE MATERIALS

Materials	Source	Designation	Poros-ity (%)	Range of Pore Diameters (microns)	Specific* Area (cm²/g)
Nickel	Micro Metallic Corp.	Ni-M	34	10–50	190
Nickel	Micro Metallic Corp.	Ni-H	40	10–30	950
Vasco 431 s.s.	Amplex Div., Chrysler Corp.	431	18	10–50	—
Silver	−80 +200 Powder	Ag-M	42	1–50	75
Silver	−200 +325 Powder	Ag-F	50	1–20	500
Gold	Powder	Au	62	1–10	340

* There is considerable error inherent in the measurement of low specific areas of small samples. Areas in the range of 100 cm²/g may be assigned errors of $^{+40\%}_{-80\%}$ at 1000 cm²/g these decrease to $^{+20\%}_{-40\%}$.

131

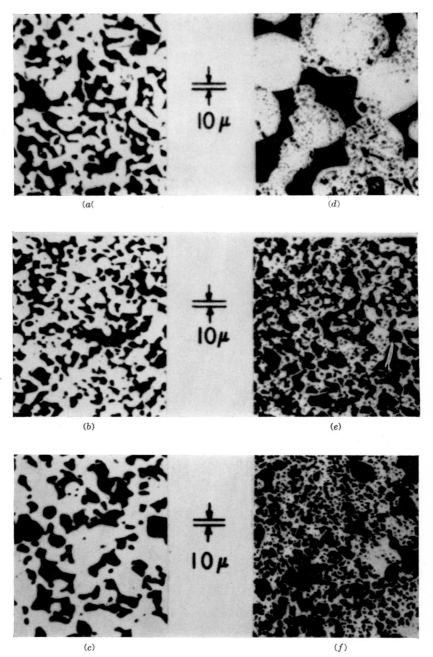

(a((d)

(b)   (e)

(c)   (f)

Figure 9–3. Photomicrographs of several porous metals used in electrodes. (100✕)

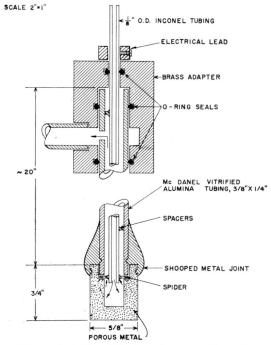

Figure 9-4. Gas-diffusion electrode, Type I.

of experiments can be seen in Figure 9-4. Positive electrical contact between
the spider and the porous metal electrode proper was made by spot welding
or brazing. The "Inconel" (stainless steel is used in some cases) gas delivery
tube then served as an electrical lead also. While the alumina tubing was
not completely resistant to attack by the molten carbonates, the corrosion
observed at 650°C over periods of a few hundred hours was not appreciable.
The porous materials used with this type of construction (Type I) include
Ni-M, Ag-M, Ag-F and Au (see Table 9-1). Flame-sprayed (Shooped) nickel
was used to attach the nickel electrodes to the alumina and silver for bonding the silver and gold electrodes. This technique of attaching the electrodes
proved very satisfactory. In calculating current densities the area was taken
as that of a surface midway between the inner and outer surfaces of the
electrode.

Electrodes of Type I proved to be unsatisfactory for carbon monoxide rich
fuels. The combination of the small inside diameter with catalysis of Boudouard's reaction by iron oxide led to rapid plugging of the gas inlet tubes

with carbon. To avert this, the design shown in Figure 9-5 was adopted. The construction techniques were first tested on smaller electrodes based on $3/8$-in. diameter alumina tubing and using hydrogen fuel (Type IV electrodes). No difficulties with plugging of the ceramic gas inlet tubes were encountered with Type IV electrodes. The adapter, similar to that used with Type I electrodes to seal the upper end of the tube and confine the exit gas flow, is not shown in Figure 9-5.

As mentioned earlier, the system contained a reference electrode. This consisted of a short length of gold tubing brazed to the usual alumina. A plug of porous gold or silver provided the active surface and a gold wire running the length of the tube on the inside made electrical connection. Since it was operated on a static head of oxygen-carbon dioxide, no separated gas inlet and exit paths were required. Figure 9-6 shows a cross section of the reference electrode. Actually the reference electrode was another cathode operated without current drain. For the purpose at hand, the important re-

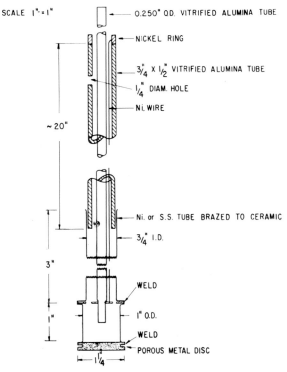

Figure 9–5. Gas-diffusion electrode, Type IV.

quirement was that the electrode exhibit a stable potential over reasonable periods of time. This was found to be the case. One electrode, used with several cell assemblies, gave the same open-circuit potential with respect to anode and cathode within ± 20 mv. This steady potential was reached 1 or 2 hr after immersion of the electrodes in the molten salt. The reason for this slow activation is not understood. When the electrolyte was grossly contaminated with oxides of iron (nickel ?), their slow deposition on the gold tube and porous plug of the reference electrode was observed. In an extreme case, the electrode became covered with a solid layer of magnetite and the potential shifted by several hundred millivolts.

Negligible polarization of the reference electrode was experienced when used with a potentiometer or a vacuum tube voltmeter. This was expected in view of the almost total lack of any but ohmic polarization shown by silver or gold cathodes (see below). One shortcoming of the reference electrode set-up was the geometrical arrangement. Ideally the reference elec-

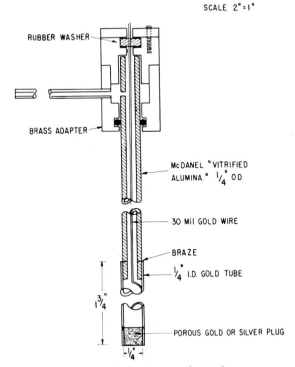

Figure 9–6. Reference electrode.

trode should be brought in close proximity to the working electrode of interest. The usual approach in aqueous systems is to use a Luggin capillary, the tip of which is placed very close to the electrode surface under study. Unfortunately, the materials and techniques required to make a Luggin capillary for use in the highly corrosive molten alkali carbonates do not exist. A consequence of the separation of reference and working electrodes was uncertainty in the polarization values. This was not considered serious, since only semiquantitative measurements were required for comparing performance of electrodes.

Reagent grade lithium, sodium and potassium carbonates were thoroughly mixed in the mole proportion 4:3:3 in a jar-mill. The mixture was dried overnight at 150°C under dry carbon dioxide. Exposure to the atmosphere was minimized thereafter and each batch of mixed salt was premelted in a carbon dioxide atmosphere before use.

In the experiments carried out so far, the fuel flow rates were maintained at from ten to twenty times that corresponding to the maximum current drawn. A considerable difficulty in specifying the exact composition of the reacting gas in the lower temperature experiments (500 to 600°C) arose because this was changed by the water gas, the water gas shift and Boudouard's reactions taking place in the electrode and gas inlet tube. The basic assumption that the gas composition did not change significantly with current in any given experiment was substantiated by two observations, namely, analysis of the gas effluent on open circuit corresponded to that on maximum current to within a few per cent and increasing the flow rates had no effect on performance. Earlier experiments were carried out with dry hydrogen-reliance being placed on the water product to saturate the gas effectively. In some later experiments, a room temperature bubbler was provided to add some water vapor to the gas. The gas pressures in the electrodes were adjusted so that bubbling into the electrolyte did not occur. In general, this pressure was about 2 psig; although many of the electrodes would support as much as 5 psig without bubbling. Since small changes in pressure had no effect on performance, the operating pressure in all cases may be taken as 2 ± 1 psig.

Results

Operating conditions and electrode details for some of the various electrode assemblies which have been studied so far are given in Table 9-2. The column headings are self-explanatory. Table 9-1 should be referred to for details of electrode materials. In Table 9-2 the operating data associated with measured electrical performance are given. The last columns refer to

Table 9-2. Cell Operating, Performance and Construction Data

Experiment No.	Fuel Feed (cc/min)				Oxidant Feed (cc/min)		Temp. (°C)	Open-circuit Voltage (Volts)	Maximum Power[a] (mw/cm²)	Construction				Polarization Curves (Figure and Curve)
										Anode		Cathode		
	H_2	CO	CO_2	H_2O	O_2	CO_2				Material	Type	Material	Type	
FCID-2	6	—	—	—	0.9	3.6	600	0.62	1.2	Ni-M	I	Ni-m	I	8A
FCIE-2	6	—	—	—	1	2.5	550	0.62	1.5	Ni-M	I	Ni-M	I	8B
FCIE-4	6-7	—	—	—	—	4.3	550	0.52	0.65	Ni-M	I	Ni-M	I	8C
FCIF-4	6-7	—	—	—		3 (Helium)	550	0.43	0.3	Ni-M	I	Ni-M	I	8D
FCIF-1	9	—	—	—	1.5	7.2	550	0.64	1.5	Ni-A	I	Ni-A	I	8E
FCIH-1	14	—	—	—	1.0	4.3	500	0.57	1.8	Ni-M	I	Ni-M	I	8F
FCIJ-1	10	—	—	—	1.4	3.5	500	0.57	1.7	Ni-M	I	Ni-M	I	9A, 10A, 10B
FCIJ-1	15	—	—	—	1.4	3.4	600	0.68	2.6	Ni-M	I	Ni-M	I	9B, 10C, 10D
FCIIIA-1	11	—	—	—	1.4	6.2	510	0.55	1.7	Ni-H	III	Ni-	III	11A, 12A, 12B
FCIIIA-1	14	—	—	—	1.9	5.7	570	0.68	5.2	Ni-H	III	Ni-	III	11B
FCIIIA-1	14	—	—	—	2.2	7.5	650	0.83	8.6	Ni-H	III	Ni-	III	11C
FCIK-1	8	—	—	—	2.2	4.8	500	1.21	14.3	Ni-M	I	Ag-M	I	13A, 14A, 15A
FCIK-1	9	—	—	Sat. 30°C.	1.4	5.5	550	1.21	17.7	Ni-M	I	Ag-M	I	13B
FCIK-3	11	—	—	Sat. 30°C.	1.7	5.1	550	1.25	18.8	Ni-M	I	Ag-M	I	13C, 14B, 15B
FCIK-3	11	—	—	Sat. 30°C.	1.4	5.1	600	1.23	18.5	Ni-M	I	Ag-M	I	13D, 14C, 15C
FCIK-3	11	—	—	Sat. 30°C.	1.4	5.6	650	1.25	19.2	Ni-M	I	Ag-M	I	13E, 14D, 15D
FCIK-3	7.6	3.3	—	Sat. 30°C.	1.7	5.7	650	1.12	19.7	Ni-M	I	Ag-M	I	13F, 14E
FCIVA-1	—	6.0	—	—	2	5	610	0.94	8.5	431	IV	Ag-M	I	16A, 17A
FCIVB-1	5.1	—	—	Sat. 30°C.	1.4	5.3	600	1.31	20.3	Ni-F	IV	Ag-F	I	18A
FCIVB-1	—	7.7	3.6	Sat. 30°C.	1.4	6.3	600	1.02	9.2	Ni-F	IV	Ag-F	I	16B
FCIL-1	7.5	—	—	Sat. 30°C.	1.9	7.8	500	1.23	8.9	Ni-M	I	Au	I	19A, 20A
FCIL-1	7.5	—	—	Sat. 30°C.	1.9	7.8	550	1.23	10.4	Ni-M	I	Au	I	19B, 20B
FCIL-1	7.5	—	—	Sat. 30°C.	1.9	7.8	600	1.23	15.3	Ni-M	I	Au	I	19C, 20C

[a] Based on anode geometrical area.

the graphs (Figure Nos.) in which the polarization behavior (over all cell and individual electrode) is plotted. Two items which have been omitted are the pressure of the fuel and oxidant gases. In nearly all cases, the pressure in each electrode was held at 2 ± 1 psig. In the reference eletrode, the $O_2 + 2CO_2$ mixture was held at a few cm (Hg)—just below the pressure at which bubbling into the melt occurred.

For proper interpretation of individual electrode polarization, it is desirable that the ohmic contribution be subtracted from the over-all polarization. This means that the internal resistance of the cell must be known. The most direct method of determining this is to use an alternating current bridge. Unfortunately, the design of the cell is such that this method did not yield reliable values. The leakage paths to the conducting walls of the crucible resulted in low values. At 600°C the measured a.c. resistance was 0.60 ± 0.15 Ω. The calculated resistance for a column of molten salt between the electrodes, using the specific resistivity given by Broers,[2] was 0.8 Ω at 600°C. An error of at least ± 20 per cent must be assigned to Broers' resistivities, since his conductivity apparatus was relatively crude.

More elegant methods for evaluating the internal resistance are based on the voltage response as a function of time on applying a load to the cell, for example. The voltage decrease due to ohmic resistance occurs instantaneously while the diffusion and activation effects require finite amounts of time. Since in these cells the diffusion effects seem to be quite slow (of the order of many minutes) and activation polarization may be expected to be negligible at these temperatures, for hydrogen at least, a fast recording potentiometer was considered adequate to measure the ohmic polarization. A Mosely Model 3 X-Y Plotter, with a full-scale pen-travel time of $\frac{1}{2}$ sec, was used. A push-button switch was arranged so that when partially depressed the cell load circuit was closed. Further depression of the switch activated the solenoid in the recorder pen-drop circuit. With practice, it was possible to record the voltage and current within less than a second after closing the load circuit. The slope of the voltage *vs.* current curve so obtained is a fair measure of the internal resistance of the cell. It was found that both CO and H_2 gave similar slopes—an indication that activation polarization was not contributing to the measured voltage drop. A few representative "immediate polarization" curves are shown in Figure 9-7. Separate experiments showed that the internal resistance measured with any one cell by this method was reproducible to ± 10 per cent; variations from cell to cell amounted to as much as 50 per cent in some cases. Accordingly 1.8 ohm at 500°C, 1.2 ohm at 600°C, and 1.0 ohm at 650°C were taken as best estimates of cell resistance.

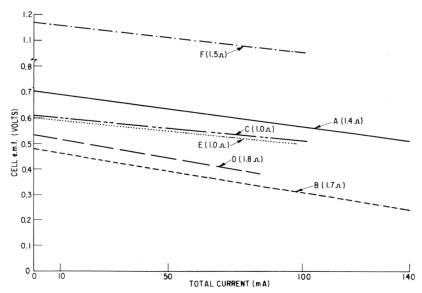

Figure 9–7. "Immediate polarization" curves showing ohmic polarization at various temperatures. (A) 630°C; (B) 640°C; (C) 600°C; (D) 545°C; (E) 600°C; (F) 500°C.

With each "fuel cell" or assembly of electrodes the primary measurement made was the polarization of the electrodes as a function of current density. The results are plotted in a series of "performance curves." In later experiments, in which a reference electrode was included, the polarization of the individual electrodes was recorded and plotted as "electrode polarization" curves. Since the results are semiquantitative only, neither the electrode polarization curves nor the performance curves are corrected for ohmic drop. However, the ohmic resistance of the cells as determined from "immediate polarization" curves is plotted in each case. This suffices for rough estimation of the electrode performance.

Results obtained with porous nickel anodes and cathodes are plotted in Figures 9-7 through 9-12. While the individual electrode polarization with these cells was not severe, the low open-circuit voltage makes them unattractive. The possible reasons for this are covered below in the discussion. As seen in Figures 9-13 through 9-20, cells with nickel anodes and silver or gold cathodes gave near theoretical open-circuit voltage. The oxygen electrode on silver (Figure 9-15) showed little but ohmic polarization at 600°C and above. This is in accord with the results of other investigations.[2, 3]

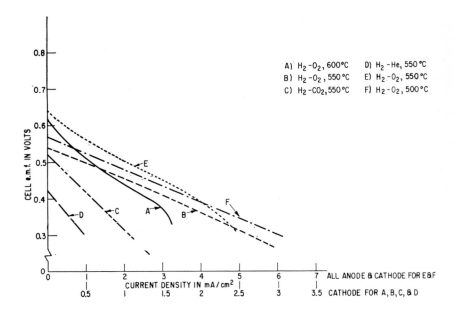

Figure 9–8. Performance curves of cells with nickel electrodes.

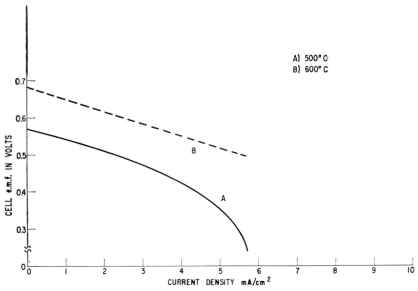

FIGURE 9–9. Performance curves (FCIJ) nickel-hydrogen and oxygen electrodes.

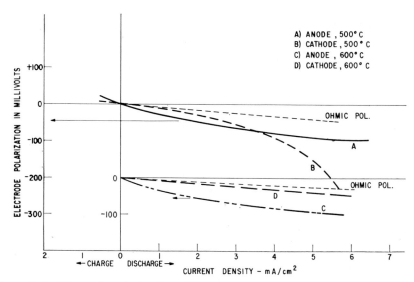

Figure 9–10. Electrode polarization (FCIJ) nickel-hydrogen and oxygen electrodes.

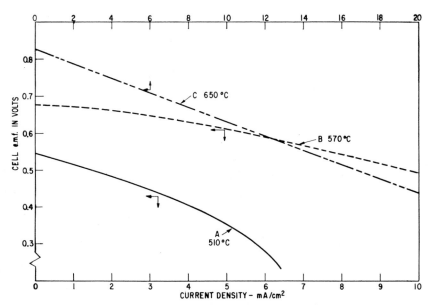

Figure 9–11. Performance curves (FCIIIA) cells with nickel disc hydrogen and oxygen electrodes. (A) 510°C; (B) 570°C; (C) 650°C.

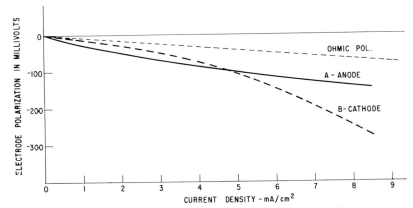

Figure 9–12. Electrode polarization (FCIIIA) cells with nickel disc hydrogen and oxygen electrodes at 500°C.

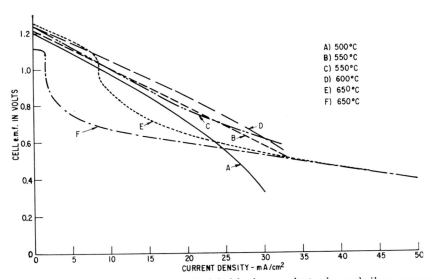

Figure 9–13. Performance curves of nickel-hydrogen electrodes and silver-oxygen electrodes at various temperatures.

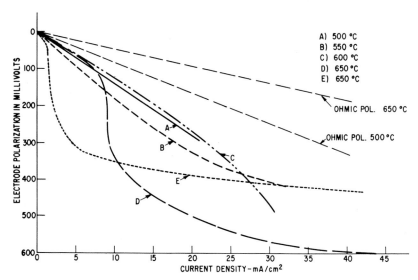

Figure 9–14. Electrode polarization of nickel-hydrogen electrodes.

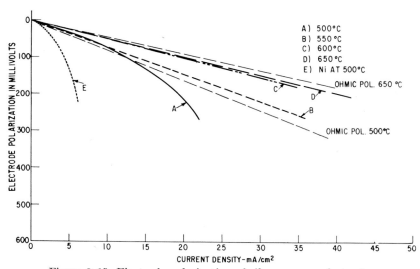

Figure 9–15. Electrode polarization of silver-oxygen electrodes.

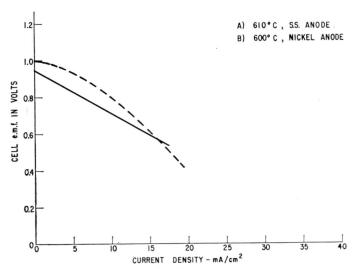

Figure 9–16. Performance curves of cells on carbon monoxide operation. (Silver oxygen electrode used in both experiments.)

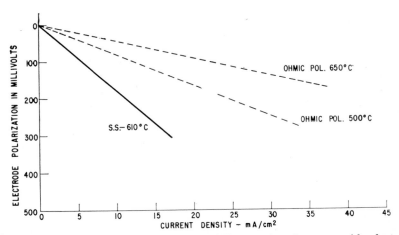

Figure 9–17. Electrode polarization of stainless steel carbon monoxide electrode at 610°C.

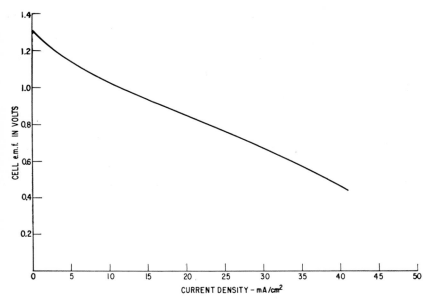

Figure 9–18. Performance of cell FCIVB with nickel-hydrogen electrode and silver-oxygen electrode at 600°C.

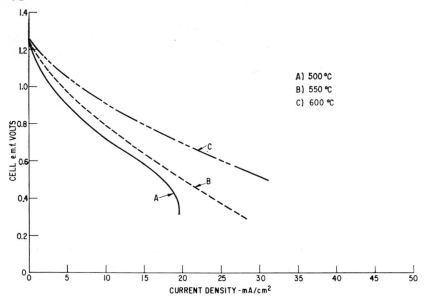

A) 500 °C
B) 550 °C
C) 600 °C

Figure 9–19. Performance curves of cells with nickel-hydrogen electrodes and gold-oxygen electrodes at various temperatures.

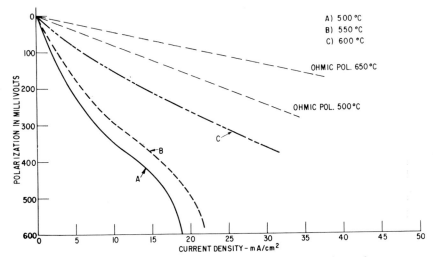

POLARIZATION IN MILLIVOLTS

CURRENT DENSITY - mA/cm²

A) 500 °C
B) 550 °C
C) 600 °C

OHMIC POL. 650°C

OHMIC POL. 500°C

Figure 9–20. Electrode polarization of gold-oxygen electrodes.

Discussion

The most striking feature of the earlier results with nickel anodes and cathodes was the low open-circuit voltages obtained (Figures 9-8, 9-9, 9-11). Even more remarkable was the fact that appreciable currents were obtained with only carbon dioxide or helium fed to the cathode. This result indicates that a cathode reaction other than the reduction of oxygen was taking place. It is likely that this reaction was the reduction of nickel oxide. A possible series of reactions is:

$$Ni + M_2CO_3 \rightarrow NiO + M_2O + CO \qquad \text{Formation of nickel oxide} \quad (A)$$

$$NiO + 2e^- + CO_2 \rightleftarrows Ni + CO_3^= \qquad \text{Cathode half-cell reaction} \quad (B)$$

Further evidence for reaction (A) is the fact that carbon monoxide was detected in the effluent gas from the cathode (a Mine Safety Appliances Company carbon monoxide detection tube was used for this). From available thermodynamic data[4] one may calculate the free energy of the over-all cell reaction,

$$H_2 + NiO \rightleftarrows H_2O + Ni \qquad (C)$$

and from this the theoretical open-circuit voltage. This is done in Table 9-3 for the temperature range of interest. It is postulated that the oxygen electrode potential was controlled by a combination of reaction (B) and the reduction of oxygen

$$\tfrac{1}{2}O_2 + CO_2 + 2e^- \rightleftarrows CO_3^=. \qquad (D)$$

TABLE 9-3

$$H_2 + NiO \rightarrow H_2O + Ni$$

STANDARD FREE ENERGY CHANGE AND OPEN CIRCUIT POTENTIAL

T (°K)	$\Delta G°$ (kcal/mole)	$E°$ (volts)
800	−9.16	0.199
900	−10.08	0.218
1000	−10.95	0.237

As mentioned above, the full theoretical open-circuit potentials for the hydrogen-oxygen and carbon monoxide-oxygen cell reactions were realized with nickel anodes and gold or silver cathodes. No precise calculations of potentials using the Nernst equation were made, since the water gas and Boudouard reactions taking place in the electrode and gas delivery tube made it impossible to specify exactly the composition of the fuel gas in the reaction zone. In addition to yielding full open-circuit voltage, it is clear from Figure 9-15 that at 600°C and above the silver cathode suffered little or no polarization other than ohmic drop. Although the results are not so extensive, it appears from Figure 9-10 that nickel cathodes did not polarize seriously at 600°C. Gorin and Recht report that, lithiated nickel oxide is an effective oxygen electrode.[3] Gold cathodes, on the other hand, suffered a more severe polarization at 600°C and below, as seen in Figure 9-20. This may be due to differences in pore size and distribution, however. More experiments are needed, but the results suggest that the unique permeability of silver to oxygen may be involved in the reaction mechanism.

As a hydrogen electrode, nickel appeared to be effective, though inferior to silver for oxygen, at temperatures above 550°C. This conclusion must be considered tentative until experiments relating electrode polarization to pore size and structure have been completed. The importance of this factor over the range of pore sizes of interest is not known, but preliminary results with silver electrodes suggest that factors of two to three in polarization (voltage drop at a given current) may be involved in going from fine pore diameters averaging about 10 microns to diameters averaging about 50 microns. The sigmoid shaped polarization curves for hydrogen on nickel at 650°C were representative of behavior at this temperature. On rare ocasions similar behavior was observed at lower temperatures. The curves strongly suggest that two electrode reactions were taking place, one predominating at low current densities and the other at higher currents. Reference to Table 9-2 shows that the main difference between operating conditions pertaining to curves D and E was the addition of carbon monoxide to the hydrogen feed. The occurrence of the inflection at lower current densities in the presence of greater carbon monoxide concentrations may mean that the two reactions were the oxidation of hydrogen and carbon monoxide—the latter occurring at higher current densities. This conclusion is supported by the argument that even with a pure hydrogen feed the amount of carbon monoxide in the electrode gas space will increase with current density due to the water gas shift equilibrium,

$$CO + H_2O \leftrightharpoons CO_2 + H_2$$

being shifted to the left. More experiments are needed to clarify this point.

With regard to the behavior of carbon monoxide at electrodes, an insufficient number of experiments were carried out to justify any firm conclusions. It appears that with stainless steel or nickel electrodes carbon monoxide exhibited about the same polarization as did hydrogen.

The electrode designs seemed equally effective. Gas tightness in the welded Type III and Type IV anodes was easier to obtain and to maintain during operation. Corrosion of cathode structures of this type was very severe when dissimilar metals were in contact with the melt and oxygen. The mechanism must be the local oxygen cell action described by Ilschner-Gensch and Wagner for molten salts.[5, 6] For nickel and silver the reactions are:

$$\tfrac{1}{2}O_2 + CO_2 + 2e^- \rightarrow CO_3^= \quad \text{(on silver electrode)}$$
$$Ni \rightarrow Ni^{++} + 2e^- \qquad\qquad \text{(corrosion of Ni)}$$

Stainless steel corroded at a lower rate; and silver coating by electroplating and/or Shooping was effective in reducing the rate. For cathode structures this is a critical design consideration, however. A further corrosion phenomenon deserves mention. Silver cathodes were found to corrode appreciably in the melt. The silver removed, which amounted to a gram or more in one hundred hours, was deposited on the anode in the form of small crystals. Some of these adhered to the anode, but most fell to the bottom of the crucible. After sufficient time, these formed a pile which shorted the anode out to the crucible. Samples of the cooled melt contained little or no dissolved silver. Corrosion took place on open circuit as well as when current was drawn. This phenomenon will be discussed in detail elsewhere. Only the shorting of the anode has limited performance. No oxygen electrode failed because of corrosion.

Evaluation

While the data are not by any means sufficient for a final evaluation of gas-diffusion electrodes, a preliminary estimate of the possibilities may be made. It seems safe to predict that power densities at least as good and probably better than those reported for matrix-type cells operating at much higher temperatures can be attained with close spaced electrodes.[2, 3] Internal resistances are certain to be considerably less with similar electrode spacings. Corrosion, if anything, is most likely to limit the utility of gas-diffusion electrodes. The investigations have turned up phenomena in this category so far unreported by investigators of cells with matrix retained electrolyte.

Acknowledgment

The author is indebted to Dr. W. T. Grubb and Dr. J. L. Weininger of this Laboratory for many helpful discussions in the course of the work. The assistance of P. R. Schmidt in carrying out some of the laboratory work is acknowledged.

References

1. Weininger, J. L., unpublished experiments, Chemistry Research Department, General Electric Research Laboratory, 1955.
2. Broers, G. H. J., "High Temperature Galvanic Fuel Cells," Thesis, University of Amsterdam, The Netherlands, 1958.
3. Gorin, E., and Recht, H. L., *Chem. Eng. Progr.*, **55**, 51 (1959).
4. Coughlin, J. P., "Contributions to the Data on Theoretical Metallurgy XII. Heats and Free Energies of Formation of Inorganic Oxides," Bulletin 542, Bureau of Mines, U. S. Dept. of the Interior, Washington, D. C. (1954).
5. Ilschner-Gensch, C., and Wagner, C., *J. Electrochem. Soc.*, **105**, 198 (1958).
6. Ilschner-Gensch, C., *ibid.*, 635 (1958)

10. Summary of Panel Discussion

Following the nine invited papers presented at the Gas and Fuel Division's Symposium on Fuel Cells, a panel discussion was held based on questions from the floor. The panel members were:

F. T. Bacon, Marshalls Flying School, Cambridge, England
G. H. J. Broers, Central Technical Inst., The Hague, Netherlands
H. H. Chambers, Sondes Place Res. Inst., Dorking, England
K. Kordesch, National Carbon Co., Cleveland, Ohio
H. A. Liebhafsky, General Electric Co., Schenectady, New York
G. J. Young, Alfred University, Alfred, New York

As there were a rather large number of audience questions of a diversified nature, it was not feasible to reproduce the entire proceedings. The following is an attempt to summarize, under three general headings, some of the major points raised during discussion. This summary, while representing opinions expressed by individual panel members, does not necessarily reflect the unanimous views of all members of the panel on each point.

Fuels

The economic feasibility of fuel cells for use in various power applications depends in part on the nature of the fuels employed. Understandably, a number of audience questions were related to the role that certain industries—petroleum companies, large chemical companies, the coal industry, etc.—would play in furnishing such fuels as would be required.

Coal, considering its ready availability in the United States, will remain a major fuel source for many years. The possibility of integrating a coal gasification unit with a fuel cell station has been one ultimate objective in high temperature fuel cell research. In such a process, the coal would be gasified either with steam to produce water gas or with air to form producer gas. These gases would subsequently be oxidized in fuel cells to produce electric energy. In order to obtain favorable over-all efficiencies, it would be essential that the fuel cells be operated at higher temperature than the coal gasification unit so that the heat developed by the cells would be available for the gasification process. If the coal gasification and fuel cell operations were conducted separately, the over-all efficiency would be little better than that achieved by the best steam cycles available today. At present

150

the major limitation to such an integrated process is the lack of an efficient, long life, high temperature fuel cell.

Saturated hydrocarbon fuels, such as kerosene, propane, etc., can be used effectively in high temperature fuel cells but again much more research and development on such cells is required before an efficient hydrocarbon-fuel cell system is ready for commercial purposes. The objective with the direct use of hydrocarbon fuels is to operate at the lowest temperature that allows reasonable current densities and does not permit excessive carbon deposition. Unsaturated hydrocarbons are readily oxidized even in ambient temperature cells.

Fuel storage might pose a problem in certain types of traction devices and other mobile or small-scale applications for those cells operating on gaseous fuels that are not readily liquefied. Methanol and other simple oxygenated organic compounds might find use as a fuel in such cases. Methanol vapor can be oxidized readily in fuel gas cells, both those operating on molten salt electrolytes and those operating at ambient temperature, and liquid methanol can be used in low temperature "direct feed" cells. Depending on the projected applications, inexpensive organic chemicals that are easily oxidized might well find extensive use as fuels.

Cell Construction and Operation

As might be expected, the majority of questions from the floor concerned principles of operation and construction of the various types of cells. Many of these questions clearly demonstrated the great need for extensive fundamental research on fuel cells and allied problems.

Present high temperature fuel cells employ molten salt electrolytes, usually contained in a porous matrix. There would be several advantages in using solid electrolytes if suitable materials could be found. Three major difficulties are encountered with solid electrolytes investigated to date:

(1) the conductivities are generally much less than for molten salts and consequently the IR drop across the cell is excessive;

(2) it is difficult to keep the solid electrolyte in an equilibrium state; and

(3) many of the solid electrolytes become highly semiconducting at higher temperatures which short-circuits the cell. The immediate prospect of finding a suitable solid electrolyte does not appear promising.

One important variable in electrode design is the porosity. In low temperature cells a proper ratio between the larger pores, which serve as the means of transport for the reactants (and products), and the fine pores at the gas-electrolyte interface, where the major portion of the reaction occurs, is necessary for optimum current densities. The upper limit on the permissible electrode surface area (primarily microporosity) thus is determined by the effectiveness of the macroporosity in allowing diffusion of the product and reactant gases. Excessively large macropores at the gas-electrolyte interface are undesirable since flooding of the electrode occurs. In high temperature cells, which employ porous metal electrodes, the porosity and surface area of the electrodes are restricted due to sintering of the metal either in fabrication or during operation.

The proper selection of electrode catalysts is another important factor in obtaining optimum power characteristics with low temperature fuel cells. A large variety of organic compounds can be electrochemically oxidized with appropriate catalysts. In cells operating at higher temperatures, the role of the catalyst becomes less important.

Future Prospects

The extent to which fuel cells will be employed in various power applications within the next few years depends on the amount of research and development work that will be expended. If a sizable fraction of the investment that has gone into atomic energy developed were put into fuel cells, the prospects for wide application would be fairly good. Small mobile power sources will probably be available in the near future. Fuel cells to power certain types of traction devices appear feasible. The combination of a fuel cell and a d.c. motor is particularly attractive from the point of view of the high torque developed at low speeds. In Germany, battery driven rail cars are competitive with diesel electrics. Fuel cells would seem to offer several advantages over conventional batteries in this area and might in time find application in locomotives, large earth-moving equipment, small ships operating over short distances, etc. The prospects for the use of fuel cells in large central power stations are unknown at present. The answer to this question as well as many others must await further developments.

INDEX

Acetylene, 27

Activation polarization, 39, 43, 62, 138

Applications for fuel cells, 21, 75, 152

Aqueous carbonate electrolytes, 27, 29

Aqueous hydroxide electrolytes, 15, 67

Bacon cell
  effect of electrolyte concentration, 67
  effect of pressure, 64
  effect of temperature, 65
  performance data, 61
  present design, 71

Boudouard reaction, 102, 133, 147

Carbon deposition, 101, 133

Carbon dioxide, contamination of KOH electrolyte, 14

Carbon electrodes, 13, 25

Carbon monoxide, 1, 29, 70, 87, 90

Catalysts, 8, 24, 30, 87, 152

Catalysts
  for acetylene, 27
  for carbon monoxide, 29, 87
  for ethylene, 27
  for hydrogen, 17, 24, 85
  for oxygen electrode, 30, 85
  for peroxide decomposition, 14

Central power stations, 4, 109

Classification of fuel cells, 4

Coal, 5, 9, 150

Commutator technique, 63

Concentration polarization, 46

Corrosion, 57, 146, 148
  of nickel oxide electrodes, 52, 146

Davtyan's electrolyte, 78, 94, 129

Deterioration of carbonate melt, 84

Efficiency of fuel cells, 5, 12, 62, 89, 103, 106

Electrode and cell geometry, 18

Electrode design, 55

Electrolyte matrices, 83, 99

Electrolytes
  aqueous carbonate, 27, 29
  aqueous hydroxide, 15, 67
  ion exchange membranes, 9
  molten carbonate, 83, 95, 110, 136

Ethylene, 27

Exchange current, 41, 64

Fossil fuels, 1

Gas diffusion electrodes, 14, 53, 130

Gold electrodes, 131

Hydrocarbons, 1, 5, 27, 151

Hydrogen, 1, 17, 21, 24, 36, 87, 90, 147

Kerosene, 9, 100, 151

Lithium doped nickel oxide electrodes, 57, 110, 147

Magnesium oxide matrix for molten carbonate electrolytes, 83, 99

153

Methane, 9, 70, 87, 90, 100
Methane reforming, 87
Methanol, 70, 151
Mica gaskets, 84
Molten carbonate electrolytes, 83, 95, 110, 136
Multistage oxidation, 105

Nickel electrodes, 53, 90, 131, 147
Nickel oxide electrodes, 52

Ohmic polarization, 18, 49, 114, 138
Oxygen electrode
    aqueous hydroxide electrolyte, 14, 21, 30, 49, 57
    molten carbonate electrolyte, 85, 96, 146

Performance data
    Bacon cell, 61
    low temperature aqueous hydroxide cell, 19
    molten carbonate cell, 92, 100, 111, 139
Permeability of metal electrodes, 119
Peroxide mechanism, 11, 14, 30, 49

pH, influence on electrode potential, 15
Platinum electrodes, 85
Polarization
    activation, 39, 43, 62, 138
    concentration, 46
    ohmic, 18, 49, 114, 138
Porosity of electrodes, 14, 56, 151
Propane, 9, 100, 151
Pulse current technique, 18

Rate of adsorption of fuel gas, 39, 118
Reaction produce removal, 18, 74
Reference electrodes, 26, 63, 134
Requirements for fuel cells, 8

Shunt currents, 68
Silver electrodes, 85, 130
Solid electrolytes, 78, 81, 95, 151
Stainless steel electrodes, 131

Tafel equation, 42
Ternary carbonate eutectic, 129, 136

Water gas shift reaction, 87, 110
Work function of catalysts, 31

RETURN TO: **CHEMISTRY LIBRARY**

100 Hildebrand Hall • 510-642-3753

LOAN PERIOD	1	2	3
4		5 1-MONTH USE	6

ALL BOOKS MAY BE RECALLED AFTER 7 DAYS.

Renewals may be requested by phone or, using GLADIS,
type **inv** followed by your patron ID number.

DUE AS STAMPED BELOW.

MAY 07 '03		
AUG 23 '03		
JUN 0 1 2006		

FORM NO. DD 10
2M 5-01

UNIVERSITY OF CALIFORNIA, BERKELEY
Berkeley, California 94720–6000